FEAR
A Ghost Hunter's Story

by

KRISS STEPHENS

Atriad Press • Dallas, Texas

Inquiries should be addressed to

Atriad Press
13820 Methuen Green
Dallas Texas, 75240
972-671-0002

www.atriadpress.com

(LCN Applied For)

International Standard Book Number 0-9740394-4-6

The editors wish to thank Alan McCuller for the outstanding cover art,
and Martha McCuller for the beautiful interior design.
We are very grateful for their contributions.

All the events, persons, locations and organizations portrayed in this book are based
on true personal accounts experienced by the authors. Any resemblance to any other
experience is unintended and entirely coincidental.

Printed in the United States of America

FEAR

A Ghost Hunter's Story

by

KRISS STEPHENS

Kriss Stephens is a master at her work, able to detect and identify minor ghostly happenings to major spiritual events. While working with her on MTV's *Fear*, she was able to determine hauntings before they had been confirmed by legend or lore. Stephens is one of the penultimate paranormal storytellers with the experience to back it up.

—Carl Hansen, Location Coordinator, MTV's *Fear*

Kriss Stephens is a fearless researcher with a BS detector like no other in the realm of the paranormal. She has worked with me in the field of cryptozoology and proven to me that she is dedicated, focused, and intent on finding answers.

—Chester Moore, Author/Cryptozoologist

Fear...it makes your heart pound... it makes your blood race... it makes your hair stand up on end. Kriss Stephen's masterpiece in *Fear* is an adrenaline rush you won't want to put down!

—Chris and Ginger Pennell, Spirit Quest Paranormal

To my grandfather, Leonard L. Williams,
for planting the seeds.

Table of Contents

Introduction

This book is about my experiences, and the experiences of my friends and family members. It is about first-hand encounters with the supernatural. These aren't ghost stories; they are factual accounts of the paranormal.

I have spent many years traveling and exploring haunted places, gathering evidence for my own research, and in the process I have encountered some amazing things. This book is a chronicle of those things, not a work of fiction. These events did happen, and I did experience them. In some cases I was lucky enough to have others with me to witness the events.

During my investigations, I've heard disembodied voices and phantom noises, seen doors slam, experienced phantom scents, and watched balls of light dance. Ghosts have thrown objects at me, pulled my hair many times, and even slashed my left arm. I've seen actual apparitions of ghosts. I've been paralyzed with fear.

I've investigated cemeteries, abandoned asylums, abandoned prisons, ghost towns, ships, castles, old hospitals, schools, battlefields, caves, mines, fortifications, and countless homes and buildings.

photograph by R. Travis Beck

I am still actively investigating. I want to understand the *hows* and *whys* of hauntings. I am no longer interested in gathering evidence in order to prove to other people that ghosts exist.

Growing up in a haunted house taught me that ghosts are real, but I will not try to convince you or anyone else that ghosts are real—you must make that determination for yourself.

All the photographs in this book are by the author unless otherwise noted. Please visit www.ghoststudies.com and www.paranormal.com for other photographs and information on these accounts and much more.

My Grandmother's House

People ask me all the time how I got started in paranormal investigation. They are usually surprised when I tell them that I grew up in a haunted house, and that I've been fascinated by ghosts all my life because of it. My grandmother's rural house is haunted by an incredibly active ghost. The occurrences are so commonplace that we've all learned to accept them as a regular part of our lives.

My grandparents built their house themselves, so I know the history. No one was murdered in it, and no one died in it.

However, there used to be an old farmhouse on the property, and we were warned to be careful in the woods on the left side of the house because an old well remained hidden out there. Much of the phenomena we experienced seem to come from those woods.

The house is two stories high, with a wooden staircase in the middle of the house that is closed off by two folding doors at the bottom where it opens into the den. Soon after moving in, we started hearing footsteps on the stairs, especially at night when we were all in bed. At first my grandparents would investigate with a shotgun, thinking someone had broken into the house.

After many late-night searches we all learned to ignore the footsteps. The ghostly episodes were not limited to night. Many times while we were watching television in the den, the doors to the stairs would rattle, as if someone were attempting to push them open from the other side. Occasionally they would open by themselves, revealing the empty staircase.

My childhood bedroom is upstairs on the back corner of the house, nearest the woods. It has two windows—one on the wall facing the side of the woods and one facing the back yard.

One night when I was about 12 years old I heard an odd creaking sound as I was trying to go to sleep. I recognized it as the sound the door on a tool shed in our garden made when it was opened. After a few minutes I noticed a reflection of a bright flashing light in the glass of the window facing the woods. It flashed every half second or so, and it appeared to be getting brighter. Soon I saw a small ball of light, about the size of a softball, move in front of that window. It blinked a couple of times, very regularly, and then passed beyond the window. I could see the reflection in the glass of the window again, and it got fainter as it continued on. Then I noticed the reflection starting in the other window; the ball of light had turned the corner of the house. It passed in front of my other window, then went a little way beyond, and then came back, passing in front of both windows again.

Gradually the reflection grew fainter until I could no longer see it. After a few minutes I heard the creaking noise again. Of course, I didn't get any sleep that night.

One of the oddest things we've experienced in my grandmother's house is the spontaneous appearance of a brilliant flash of light. For instance, on more than one occasion I would leave my room in the middle of the night to go to the bathroom, and as I opened my bedroom door and stepped into the hallway there would be a bright flash of light, as if someone had taken my photograph with a very strong flash.

It also occurred outside the house. Once when a friend and I were leaving, we were blinded by a brilliant flash of light as we walked down the porch steps onto the sidewalk. In that instance it seemed to originate from an oak tree in the front yard.

Several times while playing outside in the yard with my sister, we both heard an odd whistling noise. It seemed to be circling us, at close proximity, be we were never able to find a source.

My grandparents built a special playroom above the garage for us. It was reached by a narrow stairwell in the garage itself. It was the scariest room in our house.

We hated to play there, and my grandmother would force us to, either out of sadistic glee or frustration that they had built us something we refused to use. We had many toys in it, a desk, a table and chairs, and a shelf full of books. It would have been a great place to play—if it weren't for the ghost.

The ghost didn't want us in that room, and we knew it right away. I will never forget the dread I felt as I grudgingly walked up the stairs, with my grandmother watching to make sure that I didn't try to escape.

One of the ghost's favorite things to do was wait until we were almost to the top of the stairs and then roll something down at us, like a block or a tub of Play-Doh. It was horrifying. Of course we would run screaming back down the stairs and take our chances with my angry grandmother.

Sometimes we would actually make it into the room and warily begin to play. Then the knocking would start. This was another of the ghost's favorite tricks. It would knock on the wall, loudly, and work its way around to the next wall. Once my brother and I were determined to not let the ghost scare us off, and we ignored the knocking.

Then I watched a book fly off the bookshelf and hit the floor near my brother. That was the end of even the pretense of playing in that room. If we really wanted a toy—and we had to want it really, really bad—we would run up in teams, snag it quickly, and run back down.

When I was a teenager the activity at my grandmother's house seemed to escalate. Commonly used things, such as silverware, would disappear, only to reappear someplace odd, such as in the laundry hamper. Many times we would be using something, such as a hammer, set it down, turn to get something, and then turn back around to find the item gone. Objects would move by themselves. My sister and I watched a box of cake mix slide across the counter by itself and fall to the floor.

Soon after that incident my grandmother, my sister, and I were in the den watching television when a small ceramic swan slammed into the door to the garage, right next to us, shattering. It had been on a shelf at the end of the hall, a good 20 feet from the garage door. We were the only ones in the house.

All the other manifestations appeared more frequently, and the knocking noises seemed to get louder.

One of the funniest things involving the haunting happened around this time. I had invited a boyfriend over to visit. We were sitting in the living room, talking and watching television, when the knocking started on the walls. It went around the side, behind the couch we were sitting on, and then back along the other side of the room. He asked what it was, and I told him it was only the ghost and to pay no attention.

Then the ghost turned the television set off. We finished the rest of our visit on the front porch.

My grandmother has an organ upstairs, and my stepmother has heard someone playing music on it many times when none of us were home. Each time, she entered the house and did a thorough search, finding no one. The music would stop as she opened the doors to the stairs.

I have been married twice and have two sons, one with each husband. My ex-husbands have been the only ones to actually see an apparition of the ghost that haunts my grandmother's house. I had caesarean sections with both children, and after leaving the hospital we stayed at my grandmother's house so she could help me with the babies.

The night my first son and I came to the house, my first husband woke in the middle of the night to see a white glowing shape standing in the doorway. He said it was human-sized and that it scared the hell out of him. We went back to our house the next day, and he took a couple of weeks off from work to help with the baby.

Several years later, after the birth of my second son, we returned again to my grandmother's house after being released from the hospital. In the middle of the night, my second husband, Greg, woke to see the same glowing white form in the doorway to the bedroom. He took it a little better, and I was able to convalesce with my grandmother's assistance that time.

The ghost seems to take an interest in children. My grandmother and I were talking in her bedroom one night, and my oldest son, Aron, about 2 years old at the time, was playing on the floor with some toy cars. He stopped playing, looked at an empty space on the other side of the room from us, and said, "No, man, these are my toys," then continued to play. We asked him about the man, and all he would say was that he didn't like him and didn't want to play with him.

A couple of years later Aron fell down the stairs. He insisted that the ghost had pushed him, indeed that he felt the ghost's hands on his shoulders.

The ghost seems to take special delight in tormenting my grandmother now that she is left alone in the house. Many nights the knockings on the walls start as soon as she drifts off to sleep, keeping her awake her for the rest of the night.

Things that she needs every day are taken and returned to odd places. Her keys were once placed in the freezer. She used to take all of this in stride, until the night that something frightening roused her from a sound sleep.

She says that night she woke up suddenly, feeling terrified, and didn't know why. She hadn't heard anything, and nothing had touched her. Then an overwhelmingly horrible stench enveloped the room, gagging her. My grandmother is a strong woman and not scared of much, but she was too scared to turn and face the door to the room, where she just knew something horrible was standing, watching her.

She started to pray, and gradually the smell went away. She now sleeps in a bed festooned with rosaries, crucifixes hanging on the walls of the room, and an open Bible on the bed table beside her. She hasn't encountered that horrible stench in that room since, but she did once again in another bedroom a year later.

She opened the door and was engulfed in what she describes as an "evil smell." It frightened her so bad that she slammed the door and hurried back downstairs and onto the porch. She stayed outside a few minutes to regain her composure, then went back up to the bedroom and slowly opened the door, only to find that the stench had disappeared.

Recently she called to tell me that something really odd had happened the night before. She had been asleep when she heard a very loud thud, like something had hit the side of the house, and then she heard the sound of breaking glass. It sounded like someone had broken a window. She called my dad, who lives next door, and together they searched the house and the yard. No broken windows were found, and there was no evidence of the disturbance from the night before.

The manifestations continue to this day, but my grandmother adamantly refuses my offers to investigate her house. She says that she doesn't want me to anger the ghost and make things worse, but I think it may be because she is afraid of what I will find.

Waverly Hills Tuberculosis Sanatorium

A brief history of tuberculosis is needed in order to completely grasp the situations at both Waverly Hills and Tranquille. Tuberculosis is responsible for over one billion deaths in the last 200 years. This disease was the primary cause of death in the United States during the 1800s. TB was highly contagious, and until 1943 there was no cure. The afflicted had to be isolated in order to protect those who did not have the disease. Sanatoriums were built to house the victims of TB and those who cared for them. Many times the caregivers and their families contracted the disease from being in close proximity to the infected patients. The symptoms of the disease itself, as well as brutal experimental treatments, ensured physical suffering for the victims, along with the mental anguish of isolation from loved ones. These conditions are ripe for producing ghosts, and therefore old tuberculosis sanatoriums are among the most haunted places on earth.

I have investigated two sanatoriums—Waverly Hills in Louisville, Kentucky, and Tranquille in Kamloops, British Columbia. Both are very haunted.

Due to industrialism, Louisville, Kentucky, had a population of over 200,000 in the year 1900. The consequent boom in employment opportunities caused the population to more than double in one generation. The crowded conditions were ideal for the spread of tuberculosis, and in 1900 Louisville had the highest death rate from tuberculosis in the country.

In 1925 construction of a large complex to treat those with TB was started as the existing hospital became too small to house the rapidly growing numbers of patients. In 1926 the first patient was brought into the new building.

Due to the contagious nature of tuberculosis, sanatoriums had to be self-sustaining—basically little cities—and Waverly Hills was no exception. Many buildings were on the large hill, including stores, a power plant, schools, farm buildings, dormitories, a laundry, and a church.

Tuberculosis was a horrible disease. The early stages were comparable to a mild cold with a mild persistent cough. It progressed to where the patient had difficulty breathing and had a high fever accompanied by a flushed complexion. This ruddiness was in marked contrast to the exceedingly pale skin denoting the final stage of the disease. At this point the patient was emaciated and barely able to eat or speak due to shortness of breath and throat sores. The victim also coughed up bright red blood, and this was thought to be the vector by which the disease was spread.

At the peak of the TB epidemic at Waverly it is said that one patient died per hour. Over the years tens of thousands died at Waverly Hills.

Treatments in those days were mostly attempts to aid the patients with their breathing. The most common was simply fresh air and solariums were used for this purpose. As such, the solarium—really just large, airy, covered porches—was considered to be an integral part of TB therapy.

Patients remained in their beds and were wheeled out onto the large verandas every day to breathe in fresh air, no matter what the temperature was outside. In cold weather the patients were simply covered in more blankets. There are many old photographs of solariums showing patients covered in snow, lying in their beds. The electric blanket was invented to keep tuberculosis patients warm during the much-needed open-air treatment.

Allowing the infected lung to rest was the most successful method of prolonging a patient's life. Bed rest and positioning the patient were sometimes effective, but surgical alternatives were also used. These surgical procedures were risky and extremely painful affairs. Pneumothorax therapy involved surgically deflating the lung, therefore allowing it to rest and hopefully to heal. Another method was phrenicotomy, in which one of the phrenic nerves was crushed, resulting in paralysis of the lung. After three or four months the paralysis would gradually fade.

Thoracoplasty was also performed at Waverly Hills. This procedure involved the removal of several ribs, two or three at a time. It was used as a last resort only, with only a 5 percent survival rate.

Because tuberculosis affected so many people, medical professionals performed experimental treatments on the patients in an effort to find a cure. This was commonplace at all sanatoriums. It is not known how many patients died from the experiments performed at Waverly Hills.

The last stop for most of the patients of Waverly Hills was the morgue and a trip down the body chute, a tunnel under the property that led to the street, where a hearse would be waiting.

Tuberculosis became curable in 1943 when antibiotics were invented, and Waverly Hills Sanatorium was closed in 1961. In 1962 the facility was reopened as Woodhaven Geriatrics Center, a nursing home and mental hospital.

It's hard to find information about this period of the building's history. What is known is that the state of Kentucky closed Woodhaven in 1982, two years before the government's health-care reforms forced the closing of most mental health facilities in the United States. Locals say that Woodhaven was closed because of the inhumane way the staff treated the patients.

The property was virtually abandoned after that, although it changed owners several times. After attempts to demolish the main building were foiled by its place on the National Historic Register, one owner allowed vandals to destroy as much of Waverly as they could.

His logic was that eventually the condition of the buildings would be so bad that he would be allowed to tear down the structures. The local kids gleefully helped him out, and by the time Waverly Hills was bought by the current owners, not one pane of glass remained unbroken.

Legends of murder and suicide surround Waverly Hills, as if the bloody medical history isn't enough. Many involve the fifth floor, or rooftop area.

During the 1930s the small ward on the roof was used to house tuberculosis patients who were also mentally insane. One night the head nurse hung herself in room 502, reportedly at the beginning of her eight-hour shift, and her body was not found until her shift was over and the next nurse arrived, hours later.

Research by the Louisville Ghost Hunters Society suggests that she was pregnant and unmarried at the time.

In 1932 it is said that another nurse jumped to her death from the rooftop, just outside of room 502. And a few years ago, a man leapt to his death from the roof; supposedly he was being chased at the time.

There are tales of satanic altars in the basement tunnels, and we did see graffiti with a definite occult significance. It is said that a transient and his dog were murdered by Satanists during a satanic ritual in the building.

Several ghosts have been seen roaming the halls and grounds of Waverly Hills. One of the most active is that of a little girl with blond hair who is seen playing with a ball.

Another active ghost is the "lab coat man"; this apparition walks the second-floor hall wearing a long white lab coat. Other reported manifestations include disembodied footsteps, doors slamming, dark shadow entities, a phantom dog barking, and wet prints of bare feet appearing when puddles of water are on the floor. I experienced all but one of these on my two visits to Waverly Hills.

The remnants of a hurricane were beating down when I arrived at Waverly Hills for the first time with my friends and fellow ghost hunters Mark Christoph and James Wardrop. We were led there that night by Keith Age, head of the Louisville Ghost Hunters Society and local expert on Waverly Hills. I asked him to not give us any history of the hauntings; we like to go in without any prior knowledge so that our perceptions are not colored.

There is no electricity at Waverly Hills, with the exception of a small area on the ground floor where a Halloween haunted house is operated, so we used flashlights and LED displays to light our way as we walked through the large, ruined building.

The "draining room" was one of the first places we inspected. Legend has it that at one point in the history of Waverly Hills, patients were dying so quickly that it was impossible to prepare the bodies properly before sending them down the body chute to the mortuary and subsequent burial.

Because tuberculosis was spread by body fluids, the people of Louisville were justifiably concerned when unprepared bodies started pouring from the hill. The officials at Waverly decided to drain the

fluids from the bodies of the dead before sending them down the chute. They did this in the draining room by hanging the cadavers from poles, then slitting the bodies from sternum to groin, and allowing the fluids to drain out.

We climbed the stairs to the second floor. A main hub for the central administration areas is flanked by two wings comprised of tiered wards. The solarium stretches the length of the building, with a row of rooms and nurses stations between it and a hallway that also stretches the length of the building.

Another row of rooms is on the other side of the hall. At either end of the building are large airy rooms.

It was very dark on the second floor, without even moonlight to light up the solarium. We walked along, examining each room in turn, without experiencing anything out of the ordinary. Then we explored the third floor.

Keith skipped the fourth floor and instead we went up to the rooftop. As we stepped onto the landing to the roof and the fifth floor, we heard a door slam shut behind us, somewhere back down the stairwell. We opened the door and walked into the small rooftop ward. The rain was still pouring down, so we stayed inside the little enclosed area in the center of the roof.

The most disturbed patients were kept here when Waverly Hills was a sanatorium because the isolation made it less likely that the unhinged patients would disturb others. There is a foreboding, melancholy air to the rooftop ward; whether due to the suicides of the nurses or the loneliness and desperation of the mental patients, I cannot say.

As I walked around I kept hearing what sounded to me like small children singing a nursery rhyme like "ring around the rosy." It seemed louder on one end, in a large room that opened onto the rooftop itself. I asked James if he was hearing it too and he said yes. Mark and Keith were at the other end of the ward. James and I discussed how unlikely it was that children would be housed on the rooftop, as we tried to find a rational explanation for what we were hearing.

We walked over to Keith and asked him about it. We were surprised when he said that children were brought up onto the rooftop for heliotherapy, in which they would play shirtless in the sun. This was thought to lessen some of the symptoms of tuberculosis.

We then headed back down the stairs to the fourth floor.

About halfway down the hallway Keith turned off his flashlight and asked us to stay still for a few minutes and look down the corridor in front of us.

After our eyes adjusted we were able to make out some details due to the ambient light shining in from the solarium. Then suddenly we all saw a black shape move from one side of the hallway into a room on the other. I started to walk toward that room, but Keith asked me to wait. We watched this shape move back and forth several times, in the same general area of the hallway. When Keith led us down the hall, the movement stopped.

We went into a small room in the area of the shadow entity. Keith told us that he had been attacked by something in that room in front of several people. He had been taking electromagnetic field readings with an EMF meter and he was getting some unusual spikes in this room. He had pinpointed it to one corner when he was hit on the back with a plastic soda bottle.

Then the large overhead fluorescent lightbulb fell from the ceiling and crashed onto his head, sending glass everywhere. Just after that happened, he heard a scraping sound and turned in time to see a brick moving across the floor by itself. As he fled the room the brick hit him

on his back. This was witnessed by several people who had been standing, amazed, in the doorway the entire time.

We walked to the end of the corridor without incident, then back down to the second floor. Once there, we split up; Mark went off to the far end of the hallway, Keith and James explored the operating room and the discrepancies in the wall of the elevator shaft, and I walked along the solarium.

After fifteen minutes or so, I crossed through one of the rooms between the solarium and the hallway. In the hallway ahead of me, through the open doorway, I saw someone walk by, wearing white. I assumed it was Keith. I snuck quietly through the room, planning to scare him, but when I stepped into the hallway no one was there.

I walked back down to the operating room and found Keith and James still there; both were wearing black. A few minutes later, Mark came back. A man in white had appeared behind him while he was in the large room at the end of the hall. He heard footsteps and turned just in time to see the apparition before it disappeared. That was when Keith told us about the lab coat guy, suspected to be the ghost of an orderly who died after contracting tuberculosis while working in the hospital. He has been seen by many visitors to Waverly over the years.

I reluctantly left that night for the long ride back to Adams, Tennessee, with a strong desire to spend more time at Waverly Hills.

A couple of months later Keith contacted me about speaking at an upcoming LGHS conference. The first thing I asked was if we could go to Waverly while I was there, and he assured me that Waverly would be a big part of the conference, so I jumped at his offer. Mark Christoph came with me once again.

We arrived at the sanatorium to find over a hundred people lined up for the delicious barbecue dinner arranged for us by the LGHS. After doing some filming with Figure 8 Productions, Mark, Keith, and I joined a group of people who were exploring the body chute. We all walked down the steep incline to the end of the tunnel, then back up again.

Lots of spiders but, sadly, no ghosts. Then we all entered the main building.

I was pleasantly surprised to find that splitting up the people into groups and staggering the tours worked very well. The building was more than large enough to accommodate all of us and retain its creepy vibe. Right away people started having problems with camera and flashlight batteries draining, a hallmark of very active hauntings. We had a door slam shut just in front of us, and the shadow entity returned. This time I managed to sneak around through the solarium and come up behind the area where it was seen, but I wasn't able to see it again.

Many people experienced the hauntings of Waverly that night. One woman was even pushed back into the rest of her group by an invisible force she described as feeling like a human body.

Waverly Hills is, indeed, one of the most haunted places on earth, and I highly recommend a visit to anyone interested in experiencing a haunting first-hand.

The French Murders

In Memory of
AARON FRENCH
his WIFE and
five children
who were brutally
murdered by
JOHN HUBBARD
and his WIFE
about the 9th of
October 1855.
In Wabash Co.
Indiana.

—From their tombstone in Richvalley Cemetery

When my friend Mark Christoph invited me to Kokomo, Indiana, I was less than thrilled. I mean, who wants to go to Indiana? However, my attitude changed when he told me about the ghost of a little girl that appeared regularly in a cornfield near his friend Wendy's house, and the violent history behind the apparition.

In 1854 Aaron French, his wife, and five children lived in a cabin in Richvalley, Indiana. John Jr., the oldest child, was 13 years old, Sarah was 11, Louise was 8, and Tilman was 6. The Frenches also had a 15-month-old daughter whose name has been lost to history. Aaron French became sickly and was unable to do much work, so when a small family that was passing through offered to move into the cabin and help with the chores and garden, it seemed like an ideal way to solve their problems.

John Hubbard, his wife, Sarah, and his son, Richard, were from Fort Wayne, Indiana. They traveled to Richvalley while working on the Erie Canal and the Wabash railroad, which were both being constructed at that time. Not much was known about the family, but they seemed to be hard workers and were accepted by the small community. Certainly Aaron French seemed to trust them; otherwise he wouldn't have allowed them to stay in the small cabin with his family.

One morning a neighbor stopped by the cabin to talk to John Hubbard as he worked in the garden. John told him that the French family had left suddenly the night before. According to John, the family suddenly inherited some money and a house and had moved to Iowa. In their haste to leave they had sold most of their belongings to Hubbard for $40.

The Hubbards took in Edward Boyle as a boarder a short time after the French family left. Boyle worked on the Erie Canal, but soon he too disappeared, during the month of December. He'd been seen with a large sum of money just before that, so people assumed he had used it to simply leave the area.

Then, in March, the water was drained from the nearby canal system in order to do some work, and the body of Edward Boyle was found. It was soon determined that Boyle had been murdered, and both John Hubbard and his son were arrested and taken to the Wabash County jail, accused of the murder. John was the prime suspect, because just after Boyle's disappearance John was known to have a great deal of money.

Sarah Hubbard came to visit her husband and son in jail, and the conversation she had with her husband was overheard. In it she talked about the murder of the French family and said the family was buried under the floorboards of the cabin. She was arrested, and the local sheriff was sent to search the French cabin.

The sheriff and his deputy pried up the floorboards of the cabin. Eighteen inches beneath the floor they uncovered the body of one of the French children. Soon all seven members of the French family were found. Their skulls had been crushed and they had been placed in a mass grave—the parents on the bottom, then each of the children. Mrs. French's neck and leg were broken, and she was nearly naked. Sarah Hubbard had apparently taken Mrs. French's dress off her dead body and had been seen wearing it many times in the months that followed the disappearance of the French family.

The townspeople burned the cabin to the ground and buried the French family in the Richvalley Cemetery. A memorial was raised over the mass grave, recording the tragedy in stone.

John and Sarah Hubbard were tried for the murders of the French family and Edward Boyle. Richard Hubbard was set free after he was able to prove that he was working away from the cabin at the time of the murders.

Sarah was sentenced to life in prison and died there on January 16, 1887. John was sentenced to death, and was hung from the gallows on the grounds of the county courthouse. But his story doesn't end there.

Arrangements had been made for John's body to be sent to Fort Wayne, but when the casket arrived his body wasn't in it. Somehow his body had "mistakenly" been buried in the potter's field near the county poorhouse. These were the days of body snatching, and medical students and doctors alike went to great lengths to procure cadavers for dissection. John's body was covertly dug up, dissected, and his bones reassembled by a doctor in the town of La Fontaine, who then had the skeleton mounted and displayed it in his office for years. Later, John's skeleton was kept in the local high school. When John's body was dissected, it was found to have several bullets in it; the wounds had healed years before John's execution.

Mark and I drove out to the remote area of Wabash County near where the French cabin once stood. His friend Wendy and her family lived nearby, and they had seen the ghost of the little girl many times. They believed that she was Sarah French, because the cornfield in which she was most often seen was once part of the property associated with the cabin. She was seen wearing a white dress and was often just standing at the edge of the field, but sometimes she was seen running through it.

It was late afternoon when Mark and I were able to hike into the woods to try to find the cabin site and the cemetery. We climbed down an embankment and walked along a small creek until we were deep in the woods. We then crossed the creek and found what remained of an old corncrib in what had once been a clearing but was rapidly being reclaimed by the woods.

After thoroughly searching that area, we were unable to find any definite remains of the cabin, so we continued deeper into the trees. We jumped the creek again and hiked up a limestone bluff to discover the small Richvalley Cemetery at the top, surrounded by woods.

The memorial marker for the French family was easy to find, being a large piece of black marble with another bright white slab of marble in the center.

We photographed the entire cemetery, noting nothing unusual in the images. However, my attention was drawn to a wooded area on the other side of the small fence that surrounded the graves.

Mark went back toward the clearing to search for the cabin, and I crossed the fence and walked onto what must have once been the road to the graveyard. I walked slowly through the dense trees. Something white was moving around. I could see the movement out of the corner of my eye, but nothing would be visible when I turned directly to look. I took several photographs with my digital camera and indeed there was a pale orb in many of them, about four feet off the ground, the same height that I was seeing the movement.

I knelt down and held my hand out toward the area where the orb was. I started to talk to the little girl ghost, and soon I was seeing the movement out of the corner of my eye again. It was coming closer. A few minutes later my hand was ice cold and I could feel a slight pressure as if something was touching my hand, but I couldn't see anything. Gradually the pressure eased off, and my hand warmed up again.

After awhile I walked back down the bluff to meet Mark. He too had captured an orb in several images with his digital camera, and it was also about four feet off the ground in many shots.

We left while it was still daylight but decided to hike back out the next night.

That night a cold front came in and it stormed, so when we went back the next evening it was cold outside and the ground was muddy. The creek was high, but we crossed it anyway and hiked back up the bluff to the cemetery.

It was very cold, so we made sure to hold our breath as we did the initial digital camera sweep and for the hundreds of photographs to follow. Mark and I were both using our video cameras in infrared mode as well as taking still images with our digital cameras.

Not much was happening, as usually occurs when investigating a really cold, wet location in the dark. We walked around, shooting video and taking photographs. We would get an occasional orb or two in the images, but that was all.

This time my attention was continually drawn to the other side of the cemetery, back toward the creek. I took dozens of photographs of this area, and many of the images contained orbs but nothing spectacular.

After well over an hour we had covered the entire cemetery many times, and we were standing in the middle, taking shots at random. Mark was working primarily with video, and I was focusing on still photography by this point. I turned and took yet another photo of the area toward the creek and caught a huge blob of multicolored ecto-plasm in the image.

I shouted at Mark to shoot that area with his video camera, and I fired off a round of photographs. About fifteen minutes later I caught another mass of ectoplasm. This time it was spread out into a larger

area to the left of the location in the first shot. I caught a small portion of it in the next photograph as well.

Things died down after that, so to speak, and after about another hour we hiked back down the bluff and crossed the creek. Once we were in the clearing Mark commented that he felt like someone was there with us. I took more photographs and captured another large mass of ectoplasm in one of them.

After the successive shots turned up nothing unusual, we continued the hike back. I was ecstatic with the results we had obtained and was eager to take a closer look at the images on my laptop computer at the hotel.

Mark reviewed his video and we were delighted to learn that he did capture some of the ectoplasm on video at the same time I was catching it in my photographs. He also recorded many orbs moving about erratically.

Did I hold hands with the ghost of Sarah French? I can't say for sure. However, I do know that the phenomena we experienced and recorded cannot be explained away as dust or fog. The Richvalley Cemetery is haunted, whether by the spirits of the unfortunate French family, the ghost of Edward Boyle, or that of John Hubbard, outraged at his execution and subsequent desecration.

Castle Rising

I had an amazing daylight encounter with the paranormal at Castle Rising in Norfolk, England. The ancient keep is over 800 years old and has witnessed much over that vast span of time. Perhaps the most intriguing chapter, and possibly the origin of my sighting, involves Isabella, the She Wolf of France.

Castle Rising was built in 1140 by William d'Albini. In the intervening years it was owned by various members of royalty, eventually becoming the home of Queen Isabella, daughter of King Phillip IV of France and wife of King Edward the II of England. Well, wife of King Edward until she had him murdered, that is.

King Edward II was a less-than-ideal husband. He married Isabella when she was 12 years old, but even at that young age she soon realized that her husband preferred the company of men. The union did produce an heir, Edward the III, but the feelings between husband and wife could best be described as bitter hatred. King Edward was a cruel man and he was abusive to Isabella.

In 1327 Isabella and her lover, Roger Mortimer, dethroned King Edward II. They imprisoned him in the deep dungeon of Berkeley Castle with nothing but the rotting carcasses of dead animals to keep him company. Isabella had hoped that the miserable conditions of the dungeon, aided by the unsanitary addition of the decaying animals, would bring a swift end to her husband. She wanted to avoid murdering her husband outright, and this seemed like a convenient manner of disposal. However, Edward II managed to survive the hellish conditions for five months. This made Isabella furious. She solved her problem with what has become one of the most notorious events in the history of English royalty.

Isabella had grown tired of waiting for King Edward to die, so she and Mortimer decided to hasten the process. King Edward was seized by guards and thrown face down onto a flat surface. Then, "a kind of horn of funnel was thrust into his fundament through which a red-hot spit was run up his bowels." His screams were said to have echoed through the halls of Berkeley Castle, and indeed are still heard there to this day. He died soon after, writhing in agony.

Isabella and Mortimer's ill-gotten victory over Edward II lasted less than three years. However, during that brief time Isabella's bloodthirsty inclinations were soon evident. One man who displeased her had his genitalia removed and cast into a fire before he was beheaded.

Edward's son, Edward the III, became king in 1330. Soon after, he had Roger Mortimer put to death for his father's murder. He could not bring himself to execute his mother, so instead he exiled Queen Isabella to Castle Rising.

Isabella's life at Castle Rising was not one of deprivation. She had ladies-in-waiting, knights, squires, and every other luxury befitting a dowager queen of England. However, she was haunted by her murderous deeds and by the death of her beloved Mortimer. The mental anguish drove her to insanity. Outbursts of violent behavior caused her to be confined for the last few years of her life in the upper whitewashed rooms of Castle Rising.

She died in 1358, and legend says that on the night of her death a white wolf prowled the grounds outside the castle, howling into the night. Some say that the ghost of Queen Isabella takes the form of the white wolf and is still seen on the battlements during the full moon. Isabella's ghost is seen in human form as well, running through the halls screaming in death as she did in life during the cruel, final years of her lunacy. Her maniacal laughter is also said to echo through the ruined castle.

Other ghostly manifestations at the castle include the phantom sounds of children playing and singing nursery rhymes in the courtyard.

My encounter with the ghosts of Castle Rising occurred during a bright, sunlit day in June. I arrived at the castle with members of the Tours of Terror Ghost Tour. I was the paranormal investigator for the tour, and as this was the first tour to England, there were only six of us from the United States. Our tour was led by Tony Fallon, an expert on English history as well as an avid paranormalist.

We met the curator of the castle in the small gift shop, and I asked that he not tell us anything about the hauntings until after we'd had a chance to look around. All we knew was that something odd was known to happen in one of the rooms, but we weren't sure which one. We were given little audio tour devices and then we were led into the fortifications surrounding Castle Rising.

The castle is a ruin, but most of the stairs and hallways are intact. My audio device stopped working soon after I entered the castle, so I walked with Tony and he gave a great running commentary as we went along.

The castle is magnificent, even in its decay, but it wasn't scary. I was not hesitant to walk ahead as we explored the first two levels of halls and rooms. We then climbed a narrow spiral staircase to the uppermost floor.

I was ahead of Tony, and I walked down the dark hall a little way to the doorway of a small, whitewashed room. The room had several windows, and I remember thinking that it would be warmer in there because of the sunlight shining in. I was surprised when I stepped into the room that the air was much colder. I noticed a haze in the small room, but I dismissed it as a weird light effect from the sun shining in through the old glass of the windows.

Tony entered the room and said, "What is that mist?" That was when I noticed that the haze had actually retreated to the far wall. As we watched, the mist seemed to condense into one corner of the room, then disappeared completely.

We were both very excited by what we had just seen. I started taking photographs and Tony ran out to the tour bus to retrieve an audio recorder and non-contact thermometer. I crouched down against the far wall and waited for the mist to come back. The other members of the group ambled into the room a few at a time, took photographs, and continued to explore. Tony did some temperature readings, but by the time he got back to the room the temperature had increased noticeably.

I stayed in the room long after the others left, waiting for the mist to return. After a while I heard noises from the hall; someone was coming up the stairs. I readied my camera, and an elderly lady with a giant key stepped into the room. She saw me, and screamed.

She was one of the caretakers and had come to lock the castle. The last thing she expected to see was a ghost hunter crouched in one of the rooms. She was a little shaken up, and admitted that she was always nervous on that level of the castle.

We walked back through the castle, and as the sun started to set the atmosphere began to change. It was still daylight when I helped the caretaker lock the massive doors to the castle, but already a feeling of dread was taking hold. The castle felt threatening, and the caretaker told me that she rushed through the rooms each evening, horrified by the thought of being caught inside after dark.

We walked to the gift shop where the rest of the group had gathered and were talking to the curator. Tony looked at me and grinned as I mentioned the white room at the top of the castle. The curator smiled and said, "You saw the mist, didn't you?"

Fear

I love to scare people. I tortured my brother and sisters when we were growing up, and since then I have moved on to scaring my children and friends whenever possible. You can imagine my excitement when I was contacted by a producer for MTV's television program *Fear*.

Fear is a reality-based television show that puts a small group of young adults inside a very haunted location. They must stay at the location until all of a series of "dares" are accomplished. These dares are created at each location by the production staff of *Fear* in order to eliminate cast members. If a cast member refuses to do a dare or freaks out and is unable to complete a dare, he or she is immediately removed from the show. A cast member who completes all the dares wins a cash prize. Some of the dares have included cast members being buried alive, forced to explore old water-filled cisterns for bones, made to perform voodoo rituals involving snakes and animal remains, and attempts to communicate with ghosts via Ouija board. We've even had the cast attempt to attract otherworldly bloodthirsty creatures with animal entrails.

I was hired by the producers of the show after the first five episodes to find locations and research the hauntings. Soon after, my job description broadened to include scouting locations, briefing cast members, researching material for the dares, and appearing on the show itself.

The crew of *Fear* is a great group of people. Everyone—from the director down to the production assistants—is focused on making each episode entertaining and scary. It is a lot of fun to work with individuals who share the same work ethic I do, which borders on obsession.

The locations are fantastic. We have a budget that allows us to travel to the most haunted places I can find. The criteria for *Fear* make it a lot harder to find locations than you might imagine. Most importantly, the location must be haunted. A history of violence is a plus. Size is also an important factor, as these locations must be big enough to film two nights of investigation, and we don't like to repeat areas.

Our locations are huge, such as deserted prison complexes, mental hospitals, and aircraft carriers.

Because of my involvement with *Fear*, I have been lucky enough to spend time alone in places that are normally off-limits to visitors, such as Tranquille Tuberculosis Sanatorium in British Columbia. Working for *Fear* also opens a lot of doors for me; I have found that I am taken more seriously now that I have *Fear* listed in my credentials.

Some of the hauntings I investigated for *Fear* are discussed elsewhere in this book. Here I am going to focus on things that occurred at the actual *Fear* locations themselves.

Currently *Fear* is on hiatus. That means that while the show has not been officially cancelled, it is not in production at this time. I am keeping my fingers crossed that we will do another season. I get many inquiries about the show, and the other crew members I stay in contact with agree that it is our favorite television program to work on. Fear had great ratings, so hopefully MTV will decide to bring us back.

———————&———————

The USS Hornet

The first episode location I investigated for *Fear* was the USS *Hornet*, an aircraft carrier docked in San Francisco Bay near Oakland, California. This huge ship is an amazing place, not just because of the many ghosts on board but also because of the vessel's violent history.

The USS *Hornet* was responsible for destroying over 1,000,000 tons of enemy shipping. The vessel shot down 72 enemy aircraft in one day and 255 aircraft in one month. The first strikes against Tokyo during World War II were launched from the Hornet. She earned nine battle stars for her service during WWII. She also recovered the astronauts from the Apollo 11 and Apollo 12 lunar landings.

More than 300 sailors lost their lives while serving on board the Hornet, and the vessel also has the infamous honor of having the highest suicide rate in the Navy. There are many stories of ghosts on the ship, some experienced by sailors when the ship was still an active part of the United States Naval Fleet.

The ghost of one sailor is seen in the engine room. He was working in the room when his arm was accidentally severed by the steam from a ruptured pipe. He bled to death, and his body had been cooked by the steam when he was eventually found.

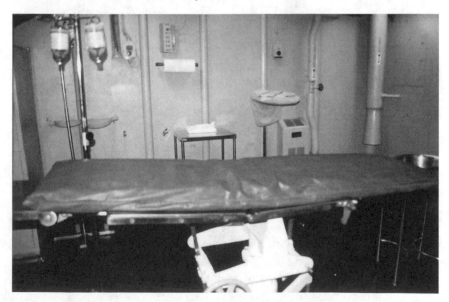

The catapult room was the site of another grisly accident. The machinery of the massive catapult malfunctioned, crushing a crew member. Just outside the room another sailor was cut in half when he tried to leap into a freight elevator.

The first thing I did upon boarding the Hornet was climb to the flight deck. The view of San Francisco Bay is beautiful, but even in the bright sunlight the deck itself is creepy. The flight deck is one of the most dangerous places to work on an aircraft carrier.

The cables used to slow down the incoming planes are prone to snapping, causing serious—and many times fatal—injuries to sailors in the vicinity. Three men are known to have been decapitated on the

Hornet by snapping cables. Other accidents on the flight deck caused fatalities as well.

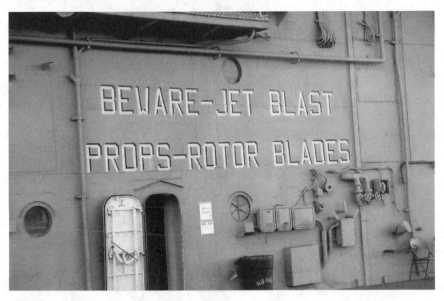

It's hard to convey how big an aircraft carrier really is. I was amazed at the size of the Hornet. It was easy to get lost in the warren of passages below deck, and most of us did get lost more than once.

The brig soon became my focus as it became obvious that it was a hot spot of paranormal activity. The brig is reached by climbing through a hatchway and down a ladder in the floor of one of the passages. Many of our crew members were nervous about working down there, and some even refused to work in that area alone.

I was able to spend some time in the brig, in the dark, and film with a video camera in infrared mode. The psychic for *Fear* was with me. She "felt" an entity approach, and while she was talking about this, I filmed an orb float into the cell, passing between two iron bars on the door. It then zoomed up and away very quickly.

Our psychic then claimed that the entity was the ghost of one of the kamikaze pilots who survived an initial impact with the ship only to die in the brig.

Later that night I was alone in the mess hall when I heard loud banging noises coming from the passage way. It startled me, but I assumed that it was one of the crew members until I walked down the passage and realized no one was down there but me.

The cast experienced many odd things while onboard. Only three cast members made it through the two nights of filming. One girl quit in the passageway next to the hatchway that led to the brig, saying she had heard noises.

Another girl quit after something caused her lip to mysteriously start bleeding while sitting in the mess hall. During her dare she had to sit in front of a thermal imaging system. In the monitor a form manifests behind her just before and while her lip was bleeding. She was unaware of this at the time, as she was unable to see the monitor. A sailor was beaten to death in a fight in this cafeteria during WWII.

As you can see, the USS *Hornet* is still extremely active, even though it now only has a "skeleton crew" of tour guides, historians, and ghosts onboard. I look forward to going back and spending more time on the USS *Hornet*.

------------ ℒ ------------

Fort Gaines

"Damn the torpedoes! Full speed ahead!"

—Admiral Farragut, Battle of Mobile Bay

The Battle of Mobile Bay was one of the bloodiest naval battles in U.S. history. During the Civil War Federal Admiral David G. Farragut led his fleet into the mouth of Mobile Bay, Alabama, with full knowledge that the waters were laced with mines, referred to as torpedoes during the

conflict. The lead ship, *Tecumseh*, struck a mine almost immediately and plummeted to the depths of the bay with most of her crew still on board. One Confederate soldier described the sinking of the ship:

> *"She careens, her bottom disappears! Down, Down, Down she goes to the bottom of the channel, carrying 150 of her crew, confined within her ribs, to a watery grave."*

As if the mines weren't enough of a hazard, the Union ships also had to withstand devastating crossfire from the Confederate soldiers at Fort Morgan on one side of the entrance to the bay and Fort Gaines on the other. At one point the decks of *The Hartford*, Farragut's ship, were said to be "awash in a sea of humanity," and so slippery from blood and gore that it was almost impossible to stand upon them.

Farragut's fleet successfully ran the gauntlet and forced the Confederates to surrender. After 19 days of heated battle and 1,822 lives lost, both forts belonged to the Union.

I visited Fort Gaines for the first time years ago, and I've returned many times since then. I am fascinated with the history of the fort and the island on which it stands.

Fort Gaines was originally built by the Spanish. Dauphin Island was known as Massacre Island during that time. The Spanish called it Massacre Island because of the piles of human bones they found on the island when they arrived. Native Americans had used the island as an ossuary for generations. Human bone fragments are still found on some areas of the island.

Local historian Don Blande is a wealth of information. He told me many interesting stories about the island and the fort, including one tragic tale involving the Native American women who had lived peacefully on Dauphin Island for generations, until the Spanish arrived.

When the Spanish first landed on the island, it was home to a tribe of Native American medicine women who were known for their teaching and healing abilities. The Spanish captured the women and forced them onto a ship bound for Haiti—and slavery. Before the ship could sail out of the bay, legend has it that the women joined hands, started singing, and leapt from the ship to their deaths in the murky waters of the bay.

To this day, the men who live on Dauphin Island will not enter the waters surrounding the island on December 16, the anniversary of the tragic event. They feel that the Native American women placed a curse on the island and its waters, and that men are the intended victims. Local residents say that sometimes on foggy nights you can hear the death song of the women.

The curse is blamed for the violent history of the island, and indeed men seem to be the ones made to suffer most. Don Blande tells the story of a girl named Catherine. She lived on the mainland across the bay and fell in love with a fisherman from the island who did business with her father. He promised to marry her after the fishing season ended, so happily she waited. The season passed and he did not return. Catherine was carrying the fisherman's child, so in desperation she chartered a boat and went to Dauphin Island to find him. Instead, she found his wife. Catherine hung herself from an oak tree on the island. Just before she tightened the noose around her neck, she proclaimed to the watching settlers, "I curse the man that did this to me and all the men in his family." Later that year an influenza epidemic swept through the settlement, killing 18 of the 20 men in Catherine's lover's family.

The land on which the hanging tree stands is undeveloped. Several men have bought the piece of property, only to die or become too ill soon after to clear the land.

It is said that on dark nights Catherine's ghost walks among the oaks to the cemetery where her lover and his family are buried. There she dances on their graves.

Cadillac Square was once the social center of the island settlement, and it is also the site where the island men executed a band of marauding pirates by hanging each and every one of them from the large oak trees.

Dauphin Island is very haunted, deservedly, and it was a great location for an episode of *Fear.* I have investigated the fort on several occasions, most recently with the Southern Alabama Paranormal Investigations group, headed by Leya Schindler. We stayed most of the night during a fierce thunderstorm. Several members of the group saw a black entity lurking in the warren of rooms on the bay side of the fort.

The black thing, as it is referred to, is the one truly malevolent haunting at the fort. Civil War re-enactors camp out at the fort, and there is one area in which they will no longer sleep. In this area several different men have awoken to something strangling them and all they could see was a black shape over them in the darkness. I have investigated this area of the fort with a psychic. She burst into tears, started choking, and ran from the room.

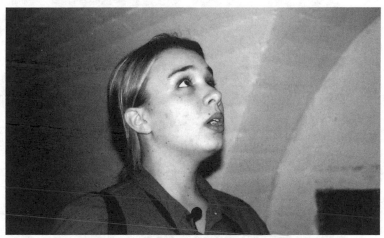

The area of the fort that the black thing seems to prefer is just behind a tunnel that collapsed from heavy shelling during the Battle of Mobile Bay, killing the soldiers inside. Supposedly their bodies are still under the earth and stone.

Fort Gaines has four bastions, built originally by the Spanish, and two of these are hot spots of ghostly activity.

To the right of the entrance is the "haunted bastion," named for the ghost of a Confederate soldier who is seen regularly walking up and down the tunnel that leads to it. I have photographed phenomena in this tunnel each time I've investigated. Ghost hunter Jeff Taylor caught streaming orbs on infrared video in the tunnel at the same time as I was photographing them with my digital camera and a SAPI investigator was photographing them from another angle with his digital camera.

The west bastion by the water has no electricity and is often flooded. During my first exploration of Fort Gaines, the batteries in my 35mm camera drained completely while I was in this bastion. I found it odd, but these things happen, so I didn't think too much about it at the time.

A couple of years later when I did the scout video for MTV, not only did my fully charged video camera battery drain completely in the bastion, but so did the battery in my cell phone, and it never again held a charge. When I got back to my hotel room and reviewed the footage on the videotape, I found that absolutely nothing from the bastion had been recorded. I had recorded for at least 20 minutes, but none of the footage was on the tape. Since then I have heard numerous accounts of batteries draining in this bastion, and subsequently I carry lots of extras when I visit Fort Gaines.

The bastion on the north bay side is where I had my most exciting encounter at Fort Gaines. It was just before the full crew arrived for production of *Fear*, and I was there with Tod Dahlke, a producer for the show, the documentary film guy, my friend and fellow ghost hunter, Rebecca, her mother, and one of her friends. We had been exploring the fort for a couple of hours. I tend to wander off by myself, and this night was no exception. I entered the tunnel that led to this bastion. It was very dark, but I could make out someone walking ahead of me. I assumed it was one of my friends until I reached the end of the tunnel, entered the bastion, and found that I was alone.

This same night Rebecca and I saw a white wispy shape move quickly along the back wall of the fort, near a gun turret.

The blacksmith shop is another paranormal hot spot, and many tourists have photographed it only to find bright white shapes in the images that they cannot explain.

There is a small apartment over the gatehouse that is so haunted that the caretaker will not spend the night there alone.

The Southern Alabama Paranormal Investigations do a yearly overnight investigation of Fort Gaines with the public, and if you get a chance to attend I highly recommend it. However, be prepared: It is very likely that you will encounter a ghost. And be sure to bring lots of batteries.

------------ ✑ ------------

Eastern State Penitentiary

"The System is rigid, strict and hopeless... and I believe it to be cruel and wrong....I hold this slow and daily tampering with the mysteries of the brain, to be immeasurably worse than any torture of the body."

—Charles Dickens, 1842

The first location I suggested for MTV's *Fear* was Eastern State Penitentiary in Philadelphia. The malicious aspects of its numerous hauntings had appealed to me for decades. My boss wasn't interested in this location at first, as they had filmed West Virginia State Penitentiary for the pilot episode, but after a month or so of listening to me beg they decided to check it out. The fortress-like buildings and thick foreboding exterior wall made a good first impression and they decided that I was right about Eastern making a great location. I was ecstatic.

We filmed in February, which was not an ideal month for shooting in decrepit stone buildings with no power in Pennsylvania. A thin blanket of snow was on the ground but I hardly noticed it as I explored the 11-acre site. Well, I did hit our psychic with a snowball, but other than that my focus was on the architecture of the place and the many ghosts.

The history of Eastern easily explained the multitude of hauntings. Eastern was built by Quakers in the early 1800s, and the first inmate arrived in 1829. The Quakers embarked on a whole new system of punishment at Eastern, based on the idea of reform through solitude and reflection. The prisoners of Eastern State Penitentiary were completely isolated from each other, with only Bibles to occupy themselves. The inmates were not allowed to whistle or sing. They were not allowed to communicate with the outside world or to speak to anyone, not even the guards, under any circumstances.

Flogging of inmates was not allowed by the Quakers, but they did implement other types of corporal punishment for such offenses as speaking, singing, or tapping on pipes. Obviously solitary confinement wasn't an option, but confinement in a cell with no windows, a dirt

floor, and no heat was. One inmate was kept in such a cell for over 40 days while shackled in irons. The prison employee who brought him food and water was fired for doing so.

Another form of punishment was the "shower bath," in which inmates were stripped and chained outside in cold weather. They were then repeatedly doused in cold water. Many times layers of ice would form on their naked bodies.

The iron gag was yet another way to torture prisoners into submission. Consisting of a 5-inch metal bar and chains connecting the bar to wrist cuffs, the bar was placed in the inmate's mouth over the tongue with his wrists behind him. The cuffs were then placed on his wrists. Struggling only forced the gag deeper into the inmate's mouth. Records indicate that at least one inmate died from this device.

Another innovation at Eastern was architectural in nature. The cell blocks each came off a large rotunda, like spokes on a wheel. A small number of guards could station themselves in the center of the rotunda and see down to the end of each cellblock.

Not long after opening its gates, Eastern was the subject of much criticism for its torturous methods. The problem was that inmates tended to go insane while imprisoned at Eastern. Charles Dickens visited in 1842 and wrote, "The System is rigid, strict and hopeless... and I believe it to be cruel and wrong....I hold this slow and daily tampering with the mysteries of the brain, to be immeasurably worse than any torture of the body."

Overcrowding forced the Quakers to abandon the solitary confinement scheme by the late 1800s. The prisoners were then crammed together in the very small cells with no regard for comfort or hygiene.

One of Eastern's more infamous inmates was Al Capone, who spent eight months there in 1929. He had a private cell.

Eastern State Penitentiary was closed in 1971. A small portion is now open for tours by the Pennsylvania Prison Society.

The crew of *Fear* was given free reign of the place, and the ghosts made their presences known to our crew early on. So did the Teamsters, but after a brief "negotiation" they limited their interaction to the street outside the prison.

Tod Dahlke, producer for *Fear*, was one of the first crew members to arrive at Eastern for the production. He decided to take some photographs with the show's digital camera, a Sony Mavica. He and one of the tour guides for Eastern were in "the hole," a dank, windowless cell with a dirt floor that was used to punish troublemakers, when Tod had an encounter with one of the ghosts.

Tod had stepped into the dark room and snapped a few photographs when he felt something tug on his backpack. He assumed it was the tour guide whom he thought had walked in behind him. He turned to see what the guy wanted and realized that the tour guide was still at the entrance to the cell and could not physically reach him. Later that night Tod went back to the cell and took some more photos. He walked to the exact spot where he felt the tug on his backpack and snapped a photograph. In it, there is a white swirling vortex of energy directly in front of him. It is one of the best ghost photographs I have seen.

photograph by Tod Dahlke

I was exploring by myself late one night, and I wandered up the stairs into cellblock 12. There are cells on either side of a screened opening in the floor that runs along the length of the block, with narrow walkways on each side. There is no electricity, so I was in darkness as I walked down the walkway. I was a little more than halfway down the cellblock when I felt something pull my hair from behind, hard. I turned and inspected the wall, thinking that maybe my hair had caught on something, but there was nothing there to explain it, no wires hanging or debris that I could have snagged my hair on. Also, it wasn't just a few strands of hair that had been pulled, but a literal handful of my hair. I turned and walked quickly back down the cellblock to the stairs, taking a few photos but mostly concentrating on getting out of there.

As I walked down the stairs I remember thinking that I needed to hang on to the handrail, because something could try to push me.

Indeed I could almost feel something behind me as I went down, making the hairs on the back of my neck stand up.

Two nights later one of our crew members was pushed down those stairs. He said he could feel the hands on his back, but of course no one was there. He quit the production that night.

Other unusual things happened as well. A large block of stone fell from the top of a wall, barely missing one of the crew members. Our computer system crashed during filming, and several cameras malfunctioned mysteriously. The ghosts seemed determined to avoid performing for the cameras, but the cast reported hearing voices, footsteps, and doors slamming while at the location.

Eastern had definitely lived up to its sinister and infamous reputation. If you get a chance to explore this amazing building, even if it is just the small section shown to tourists, I highly recommend doing so. Take lots of photographs; there is a good chance that you might be surprised with the results.

Tranquille

Tranquille on the Lake, near Kamloops, British Columbia, has more ghosts than any other place I've investigated. The huge, deserted former tuberculosis sanatorium overlooks Lake Kamloops, and is intentionally isolated from civilization. The place is hauntingly beautiful when the sun is shining, but after dark the atmosphere changes.

Many legends surround Tranquille, such as tales of the extensive tunnel system reaching all the way into the city of Kamloops and a secret entrance to the tunnel system beneath the lake. There are also tales of satanic nurses, murderous beast-like patients, and torturous medical experimentation.

I touched on the horrors of tuberculosis in my Waverly Hills account, so I will not go into them again here. As if the rigors of the disease were not enough, abuse of the patients was rampant at Tranquille. Recently a fund was set up by the British Columbian government to pay damages to survivors of victims of abuse at Tranquille. Suffice it to say that if dying horribly and suffering is part of the recipe for making a ghost, Tranquille should have thousands.

Fear

Tranquille was built in 1908 and was used as a long-term care facility for tuberculosis patients until it was closed in 1958. It reopened a short time later as a home for the mentally handicapped, closing permanently in 1985. During and after World War I, injured soldiers were sent to Tranquille to convalesce.

Tranquille is truly a ghost town. Paved roads with streetlights wind among over fifty buildings, most of which are connected by a vast network of tunnels, a necessary feature due to the harsh winters. The sanatorium was self-sufficient, with its own power plant, farm, dairy complex, and schools.

I love abandoned buildings, so Tranquille was a delight for me. I took hundreds of photographs as I explored the old buildings and tunnel systems. I was surprised to find that much of the furniture and equipment remained in the buildings.

The first building the *Fear* crew told me about when I arrived at Tranquille was the bathroom house. Tranquille only has running water in one building, a small, unassuming house where we used the bathroom. It soon became obvious to the crew that the bathroom house was haunted. They would hear footsteps and knocking noises while in the bathroom, as well as the sound of doors slamming.

There was no electricity in the bathroom house, or most of Tranquille for that matter, which added to the creepiness of late-night trips to utilize the facilities. Some of the crew members started going to the bathroom in groups so that someone could stand guard at the bathroom door.

I did a cursory initial investigation of the house, taking EMF readings and dozens of photographs, but came up with nothing out of the ordinary. Crew members continued to experience phenomena, but I was unable to detect it.

The night before we left British Columbia, four crew members went to the bathroom house together. They walked through the kitchen to the bathroom, noting nothing unusual. However, when they came back through the kitchen on their way out, they were startled to see that all the cabinet doors were opened and all the drawers were pulled out. They ran back to meet the rest of us, and I went back and photographed the house again, this time getting a small orb in one photo.

I explored Tranquille during my first night at the location with one of the producers, the documentary film person, and our psychic. A large building used as a dormitory was our first stop. It is apart from the other buildings, and was used to house the soldiers from World War I. The building was in bad shape and had bats living in it. The "angel of death," the ghost of a satanic nurse, is said to wander the halls here. I photographed phenomena in one of the hallways, and our psychic "felt" the entity wrap its arms around her.

We explored the hospital next, including an operating room that still has some of the surgical equipment remaining. One of the experimental tuberculosis treatments at Tranquille involved piercing a patient's fluid-filled lungs and then inverting the patient so that the fluid would drain out, an extremely painful and uncomfortable procedure. This apparatus was still in place.

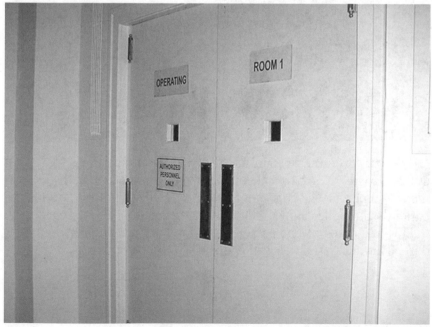

Next we entered the tunnel system.

We walked to a dead end, with me photographing the entire way, and started to film our psychic and her impressions. After a few minutes we heard a low moaning sound coming from the tunnel behind us. I turned and took a photograph with my digital camera; a cluster of orbs appeared in the image.

I continued to take photographs, and in them you can see the cluster recede down the tunnel.

No anomalies had been present in my photographs as we walked down the tunnel, kicking up dust as we went. We heard the moaning several times as we filmed the psychic.

Later that night another member of the crew radioed in to see who was in the tunnels trying to scare him. He was surprised to learn that we were all accounted for, because he had been hearing loud moaning noises coming from the tunnel system.

After we finished filming the psychic, we took the tunnels back to the Greaves Building, and then crossed the courtyard to a building that had been used as an orphanage at one point.

This was supposed to be one of the most haunted buildings on the property, and we explored each floor. A tiny sock, a creepy broken doll, and murals of storybook characters were poignant reminders of the children who lived their often very brief lives here, isolated from their families.

The attic of this building was reportedly once the domain of Pig Man, a tragic character who was stricken with lupus, not tuberculosis. Lupus horribly disfigured him, and it was said he was isolated from the contagious TB patients by being housed in the attic. Legend says that he went insane, either from his medical condition or the isolation. His ghost has been heard shuffling around the attic rooms.

After we left the building I photographed the exterior of the build-ings, and was amazed by the phenomena in some of the images. Huge clusters of orbs appeared in some of the images, without relation to the air currents.

The next day I did more exploring, taking hundreds of photographs with both my digital camera and my 35mm camera. I wandered into the Sage Building, which was a school for tuberculosis patients.

I was in a second-floor classroom when I heard a door slam shut somewhere behind me. I walked out in time to see a door at the end of the hallway slam shut.

I ran to see if I could find out whom or what had closed the doors, but I didn't see anyone or anything. As I left, two large owls flew off from their nest under the roof of the building.

I explored Centennial Hall next, with its huge kitchen area. All the stainless steel equipment still remains where was when it provided food for over a thousand patients a day.

Next I went to the pink Art Deco Fire Hall. The fire truck was still there.

After lunch I walked down to the farm area of Tranquille. This complex has many buildings, including a dairy, blacksmith shop, a huge main barn, numerous sheds, and a large slaughterhouse set back from the rest of the buildings.

I encountered something here I cannot explain and that still freaks me out to this day.

I had walked through the entire barn complex, entering each building and taking photographs along the way. Other than a few orbs in the images, there was nothing remarkable.

However, looking back I realize that I was uncomfortable in that area, because rather than explore every nook and cranny of the buildings, as I had with most of Tranquille, I would do a quick walk around, snap some photographs, and then leave.

After examining a large shed, I crossed a cattle guard that led between two pastures and continued on the gravel road to what I now know was the slaughterhouse.

This building is very quaint, not utilitarian at all, and I remember trying to figure out its purpose at the time. However, this building made me uncomfortable too, and after getting no phenomena in my images I decided to head back through the main barn area.

Tranquille is beautiful, and that area in particular has a nice, pastoral look, so I took even more photographs than I had before, including an awesome cloud formation over the hills surrounding the complex. It was late afternoon, and the sun was still shining.

When I reached the cattle guard, I decided to photograph the main barn area framed by the trees on either side of the cattle guard. I took the shot, and the resulting image was very dark.

I checked my camera settings, and they were at the default, which I had been using all week. I took another photograph, and it too was dark.

I remember thinking "Great, this camera is only a couple of months old, and it's malfunctioning." So I took a photograph behind me, and that image was fine, lit brightly by the sun.

I took another one in front of me, and it was even darker than before. I took another one behind me; it was fine.

his confused me. Why would the images in the photographs behind me be okay but the ones in front of me too dark? I changed the flash settings on my camera to manual, and took a photograph in front of me. It was extremely dark, but then I noticed that the reflectors on the tractors in the shed were reflecting the light from my flash.

I walked across the cattle guard and into the main barn area, and starting taking more photographs. All the images in front of me were dark, while the ones behind me were normal. I took some to the sides of me; they were lighter than the ones in front of me but still dark. I placed the camera on top of my head and took a shot; the resulting image is black, with several orbs in it.

I took dozens of photographs as I slowly walked through the barn area. I reached the gate to the main road and walked across that cattle guard. I took a photograph in front of me and it was brightly lit by sunlight. Took one behind me, and it too, was brightly lit. Whatever it was that caused my images to be dark was gone.

When I reached the rest of the crew, I showed the images to our head cameraman. He examined my camera and spent a lot of time inspecting the photographs from the barn area, even taking a few test shots himself. He was unable to explain the dark images.

The next day I went back to the barn area with another crew member, but nothing unusual appeared in any of the photographs we took.

A couple of months ago I came across an account from a former security guard at Tranquille. In it he told of seeing a dark mass, described as a "dark liquid blanket" that "swirled and churned." Could this be the same entity that I encountered?

Tranquille exceeded my expectations, both as a fantastic place to explore and as an active haunting. I intend to return and stay as long as I can to investigate and document its many hauntings.

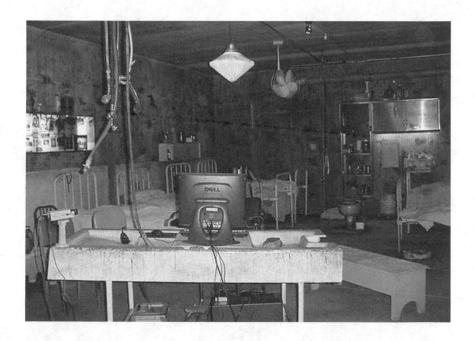

Other Fear Locations

All of the locations used on MTV's *Fear* are haunted. While my personal experiences with the hauntings are limited to just a handful, the other locations are just as interesting. I intend to revisit most of them and spend more time investigating. Here are some highlights from a few of these locations.

Desert Plantation aka LaGuerre Plantation, is in Woodville, Mississippi. We had scouted just about every plantation on the Mississippi River by the time I drove up the winding gravel road to Desert. I caught a glimpse of the white building through the massive oak trees and knew immediately that this was our location.

The large white building sits on several hundred acres of forest and has been owned by the same family for generations. There are several slave cabins still standing on the property, with the ruins of many others scattered among the trees.

There is a small cemetery near the main house, and a larger one in the back, overgrown with vines and small trees.

The land itself is beautiful, with a small waterfall on the creek that runs through the property.

A large, deep ravine lies directly behind the main house. This is where Virginia Metcalf died. Distraught after her fiancé abandoned her, she took a handful of pills and stumbled into the ravine, falling to her death. Her ghost has been seen in the ravine itself and on its banks.

The doors in the main house swing open and slam shut by themselves, and objects seem to move around of their own accord. The building was used as a yellow fever hospital at one point, and it is thought that the haunting may originate from that time period.

One of the most colorful characters in the history of Desert Plantation is Kity Pate. Kity was a slave on the plantation, and she was also a powerful voodoo priestess. So powerful, in fact, that the family grew frightened of her and set her free. She decided to stay in her cabin on the plantation, and while the family secretly wished she would leave, they didn't dare force her to. She remained there until she died, and she is buried in the overgrown cemetery in the woods behind the cabin.

While alive, Kity was known for her healing concoctions, as well as potions and charms with more sinister connotations. No one crossed Kity while she was alive, and many locals are still wary of encountering her spirit now that she is dead.

I recommend Desert Plantation as a great alternative to The Myrtles, the famously haunted plantation house in St. Francisville, Louisiana.

Desert is located 18 miles to the north of St. Francisville. Bill and Willia Perkins, the owners of Desert, are gracious hosts and make you feel right at home. You are free to explore the entire plantation, both house and grounds, and you can take as many photographs as you like.

Fairfield Hills State Hospital, also known as St. Agnes Hospital for the Chronically Ill, was the location that convinced many *Fear* crew members that ghosts are indeed real. The ghostly activity level behind the scenes was intense, with many camera malfunctions, weird electrical problems, and physical encounters with ghosts.

One producer actually saw a glowing human-shaped figure. One of the cameramen encountered a dark shadow-like apparition in the tunnels.

Fairfield is located in Newtown, Connecticut. At one time the hospital housed well over 4,000 patients. The main buildings were opened in 1932, and the facility was closed in 1995.

One of the most amazing ghostly experiences at Fairfield was told to me by one of the producers. It happened just before the main crew arrived, and the producer was walking through one of the main buildings with a couple of local people and a camera guy. There was no power in the building. As they made their way down one of the dark hallways, an old-fashioned fire alarm right in front of them started to go off. It scared them, but they stayed long enough to verify that there was no power going to it. Then they double-checked the power lines in the basement. It was indeed dead.

During the filming of the show itself all but one cast member quit because of the intensity of the hauntings.
Paia Sugar Mill, also known as Ki Sugar Mill, is located in Maui. It was built in 1875 and remained in use for 125 years before it was finally closed. The facility has witnessed more than its share of tragedy, starting with its unlucky placement on top of a burial area and continuing with recent murders and disappearances in the vicinity of the buildings.

The two most active hauntings are that of a ghostly woman in white and the screaming heard coming from the tunnels, believed to be the ghosts of Chinese workers who were killed during its construction.

Fear

The Lemp Brewery, also known as Boettger Brewery, is haunted by several ghosts that are believed to be tied to its sordid and very tragic history. In 1864 William Lemp built the largest brewery in St. Louis, Missouri. It was very successful, and the Lemp family made a fortune.

Then tragedy struck. William's favorite son, Andrew, died of heart failure at the age of 28. William blamed himself for overworking Andrew, and he became a recluse, avoiding other people by using the vast cave system connecting the mansion to the brewery to walk back and forth late at night. Then, in 1904, three years after Andrew's death, William shot himself.

Soon after William's suicide, his sister Elsa shot herself with a revolver.

William Lemp Jr. inherited the business, and at first he seemed to overcome the turmoil surrounding his family. He married Lillian Handlan in 1899. She was called "Lavender Lady" because that was her favorite color, and she dressed in lavender.

Her spending upset William Jr., and he soon divorced her. Lillian withdrew from society. William remarried, but soon his mannerisms started to resemble those of his dead father. He began to abhor dealing with people, and would travel the cave system to avoid meeting them, just as his father had done. Prohibition put an end to the brewery, and to William Lemp Jr. He shot himself in the chest with a revolver.

Charles Lemp, William Jr.'s brother, continued to live in the mansion for years after his brother's death. Then in 1949 he too committed suicide. He took his dog down into the basement of the Lemp mansion, shot the dog with a pistol, and then shot himself.

The Lemp family line died with Charles Lemp.

The house was abandoned until the 1970s, when it was bought and remodeled by Dick Pointer. The Pointer family was the first to publicly discuss the ghosts of the Lemp mansion. The Pointers opened a restaurant in the mansion, and the hauntings continue to this day with such manifestations as ghostly voices, doors slamming, the piano playing by itself, and doors and windows opening by themselves.

The ghost of Lillian Lemp, the Lavender Lady, is seen wandering the mansion, most commonly on the staircase.

The caves between the brewery and mansion are also haunted, and it is believed that a schizophrenic relative of the Lemps was kept isolated in the caves. Screams are heard coming from underground, and the apparition of William Lemp Sr. has been seen lurking in the caverns.

We captured the most phenomena on camera at Minos Dos Estrellas, in Tlalpajahua, Mexico. Minos Dos Estrellas is an abandoned gold mine located in south-central Mexico. In 1937 500 mine workers were killed when part of the mine collapsed during a flood.

However, part of the mine is still accessible, and there are numerous old mine buildings and houses still standing.

Not only is the area considered to be haunted by the souls of the dead miners, but it also thought to be cursed by the presence of a Nahaul, a shape-changing creature sort of like a werewolf. This creature was blamed for the many accidents and deaths that occurred well before the tunnel collapse dealt the final killing blow to the mine.

The ghosts made their presences known as soon as the crew arrived, with numerous equipment failures. Soon the crew was hearing odd noises such as doors slamming and voices coming from deep within the mines.

The safe house (the place were the cast stays during the day) was located inside the mine itself. Half of the cast quit during the first night of filming. The next day we caught an extraordinary event on camera. It started when the remaining cast members began complaining that it was getting cold in the safe house.

They can be seen on camera putting on sweatshirts and huddling under blankets. After a few minutes their breath became visible, and it was obvious that the temperature was dropping. This was summertime in Mexico and the outdoor temperature was anything but cold.

Suddenly one of the cast members noticed a glowing light on a far wall of the mine that stayed visible for several minutes.

Later that night something else amazing happened that was also caught on video. The lights in the safe house went out, along with the power to the computer. Just as this happened a dark shadow moved between the camera and the girl in the safe house.

The activity was so intense during the filming of that show that the entire cast quit. Another full cast was brought in and the dares were adjusted. The ghosts seemed to have calmed by the time the replacement cast arrived, and the show was completed.

Holt Cemetery

I have always like cemeteries, but purely for aesthetic reasons. Rationally, cemeteries should be the least likely place to find ghosts; people don't usually die in cemeteries, and most people don't have fond memories of cemeteries and thus have little reason to be obsessed with them.

Aside from places like Big Woods Cemetery (see the following account), those with ties to satanic worship, or some other extenuating circumstances, I thought investigating the average graveyard down the road was a waste of time. I was wrong.

Ghosts do hang out in cemeteries. One theory about why some ghosts stay with their mortal remains is that they are dead Christians waiting for Judgment Day. As a matter of fact, I know one unscrupulous ghost hunter who regularly blows a trumpet in cemeteries, then quickly takes photographs. He does get results this way, but I don't recommend his method.

Some of my best ghost photographs and video are from cemeteries. Now I photograph graveyards whenever I get the chance, no matter how small or unassuming they may be.

There is a cemetery in New Orleans that definitely falls into the "extenuating circumstances" category. Holt Cemetery, on City Park Avenue, has been used in rituals by local voodoo practitioners for decades.

You can always find melted candles and offerings near one giant oak tree, known as the Voodoo Oak. Recently it was hit by lightning in the exact spot where an offering had been nailed to the tree earlier that week.

I have found ritual drawings, or *vevres*, carefully laid out in corn-meal on the ground on some of the graves. The letters "RIP" when spelled out in flour on a grave take on a sinister meaning. It is said that if you kill someone with voodoo it is likely the ghost of that person will haunt you unless you make offerings to the loa and the ghedde of the cemetery, including "RIP" or "rest in peace" in flour on your victim's grave. I have seen this twice in Holt Cemetery.

Unlike most New Orleans cemeteries in which the graves are all in aboveground vaults, the dead of Holt Cemetery are buried in the ground.

But the dead don't seem to want to stay buried. Each of the frequent rains produces a new crop of human bones that rises to the surface with the help of the high water table. I have literally kicked over human femurs and once sent a human jawbone clattering down the small gravel road through the graveyard. The cemetery contains mostly poor people, and the headstones, when present, are usually homemade. Some are quite colorful.

Recently Save Our Cemeteries, a New Orleans group dedicated to preservation, has started tidying up Holt. I liked it much better before the restoration when the cemetery was still in its natural state, with the high grass touching the low-hanging Spanish moss.

Holt Cemetery is one of the more dangerous places to investigate at night in New Orleans, although to be honest most of New Orleans is unsafe at night. However, Holt is located near one of the higher crime areas of the city. I investigate it at night, but I do not recommend that anyone else does. You never know what might be hiding among the oaks, physical or metaphysical.

Jeff Taylor, a close friend of mine, learned this the hard way. He used to be a skeptic. That changed the night he went with me to Holt Cemetery.

We parked at the entrance and started walking systematically from the front to the back of the graveyard. I took lots of photographs with my digital camera as we explored each section.

This was before the "clean-up," so some areas were covered in tall, soft grass, while others had natural piles of leaves. There was a slight breeze, and the long Spanish moss hanging from the oak trees swayed with the wind, its movement startling me more than once as I caught it out of the corner of my eye.

I noticed that Jeff was lagging behind me more than usual, but I didn't think too much of it. I was getting some phenomena in my photographs and I focused on tracking some of it from frame to frame.

After an hour or so the manifestations died down, and we decided to leave. By this time we had walked all the way through the graveyard, and we were coming back along the gravel road near the fence and the small caretaker's shack.

When we reached the gate I had a very strong feeling that something wasn't right. Normally I try to discount or ignore these kinds of impressions, but I remember thinking that whatever this was seemed determined to frighten me.

No matter what your belief system, it is always best to be on the safe side when leaving a cemetery where voodoo is practiced and ask any ghosts that may be hanging around to stay. I did this, audibly, and the creepy feeling went away. I then went about putting up my camera equipment. Jeff started the car and we left. Looking back, I now realize that Jeff hadn't said anything during that whole process. He is normally a quiet person, so at the time I didn't even notice.

It wasn't until we pulled onto City Park Avenue that I realized Jeff was behaving oddly. He wouldn't look at me or speak, and he was gripping the steering wheel with both hands. He began to drive really fast through the city streets, which is not like him at all. He is usually a very cautious driver. I said his name out loud, and finally he turned to look at me.

His facial expression was completely alien to me. This was not the Jeff I knew. It startled me, but then I began talking to him in a very calm voice, saying his name repeatedly. He seemed to relax a little, and by the time we got home he was almost back to normal.

I had him take a bath to help him mentally "wash off" anything that might still be attached to him. When he finished his bath, he told me about his experience.

Here, in Jeff's words, is what happened to him that night:

"Toward the front of the cemetery there are a few oak trees, one of which is the Voodoo Tree. We took a few pictures around the tree and then started walking toward the other clump of trees.

As we got closer to these trees, a feeling of dread started to come over me. We started to hear a creaking noise, like some of the branches were about to snap.

I told her that I felt uncomfortable and that we needed to leave that area.

We did so and started walking around other parts of the cemetery. The rest of the cemetery was mostly quiet, except for the feeling of someone following me.

Being the skeptic that I was, I pretty much dismissed it. But after a while, I began to think that this would be a prime time for a ghost to prove to me that they existed. So, I began to concentrate on the feeling that something was following me.

The more I thought about it, the stronger that feeling got. I figured that I was just starting to creep myself out, but nevertheless I continued to concentrate.

Kriss and I decided that it was time to leave, and so we headed for the truck. After we passed the metal gate, the feeling started to depart. I wasn't about to let this happen. I began to concentrate harder on that feeling and sure enough, it came back.

We got into the truck and began to leave. I was driving. After a few minutes, my feelings started to turn dark. I began to feel violent and wanted to cause harm to others.

At one point, we came across a police car and I just wanted to get the hell away from him. That's not like me. We got on the interstate and I began to drive fast and wanted to cause terror to the vehicles around me. For those that don't know me, I'm a cautious and safe driver. I do not like to take chances.

*Kriss started asking me if I was okay and questioning me.
I really didn't want to speak to her, but I forced myself after
some time to tell her what I was feeling. She told me that my
face had changed and that I didn't look like myself anymore.
This lasted the whole way home, which is about a 30-minute
drive. When we got home, she forced me to take a bath with sea
salt. I began to feel more like myself, but that feeling of being
watched lingered for several days.
This event opened my eyes."*

Jeff wanted proof, but I think he got more than he bargained for.

Big Woods Cemetery

Big Woods Cemetery, near Edgerly, Louisiana, has struck fear in the hearts of generations of local children, including me. I grew up in Vinton, Louisiana, just a few miles from Big Woods.

Exploring during the day isn't so bad, but after the sun sets the atmosphere undergoes a dramatic change, and the large cemetery takes on an ominous, foreboding air.

Big Woods Cemetery is in the middle of a huge tract of forest. The graveyard was established in the 1820s, soon after the Antioch Primitive Baptist Church was built. I remember the church, but it is no longer there, having burned to the ground in the 1990s. The cemetery consists of two sections, each covering several acres, connected by a small gravel road through a wooded area with a cattle guard at each end.

Many a careless or slightly hysterical ghost hunter has tripped crossing those cattle guards in the dark.

Legends abound about Big Woods Cemetery: A homestead once stood near the entrance, where supposedly a man murdered his wife and children with an ax, then escaped to Mexico.

There is a "lost" section of the cemetery, somewhere in the woods, where a regiment of Confederate soldiers is buried.

Another legend is that of a "black shadow entity" that lurks on the small gravel road between the two sections of the cemetery. Stories are told that seeing this entity condemns you to certain doom.

The most persistent rumor concerns "devil worshippers." They are said to hold ceremonies in the cemetery, making sacrifices of animals to Satan, and some say the Satanists are the ones responsible for burning the old church down. These rumors are based on fact.

Animal sacrifices have been found in Big Woods Cemetery. Sometimes the carcasses are found hanging from trees; sometimes they are arranged ritualistically on certain gravestones. Usually dogs and cats are the sacrificial victims, with an occasional chicken thrown into the mix.

Graves are desecrated in other ways by the cultists, including the destruction of headstones and grave robbing. The caretakers often find the smoldering remains of small fires in the cemetery. Big Woods Cemetery is big and very isolated, and it is impossible to see most of the cemetery from the main road.

Big Woods Cemetery isn't the only local graveyard that is used by Satanists for ritual purposes. A small, poor cemetery near Big Woods, on private property, has been the site of many grave robberies, as has a small private cemetery in the nearby town of Sulphur. At this particular graveyard several bodies were exhumed by cultists, the heads removed, and the bodies hung from tree branches.

There is, indeed, at least one active group of Satanists in the area, and they do use the cemeteries, including Big Woods, as locations for their ceremonies.

My personal experiences with Big Woods Cemetery are many, starting with several aborted attempts to investigate it at night when I was a teenager. Sometimes my friends and I wouldn't even make it out of the car. Other times we would cautiously walk around the gate and walk several yards into the cemetery, only to run back to the car and leave as fast as we could.

Once we were accompanied by three carloads of football players from Westlake. They made it several yards in, and then they too ran out.

The cemetery can be a very scary place. A close friend of mine, Gary Breaux, and I tried our luck one night, only to chicken out before getting out of his car. We turned the car around and drove off.

Just as we turned off Big Woods Cemetery Road, a bright light came up quickly behind us. We both thought it was a motorcycle or a car with one headlight. It followed us a short distance, then disappeared. We turned back around and drove back to the cemetery road; there was no vehicle there and no place for one to have turned other than the cemetery road. I later found out that many people have seen this light.

Now that I am older, I have conquered my fear of Big Woods, and I return often as it is one of the most paranormally active places that I've investigated. The location is notorious, however, and it isn't unusual for me to surprise other ghost hunters in the cemetery.

I consistently capture phenomena in both my still photographic images and with infrared video. There are several "hot spots" that provide reliable results. I have a very creepy photograph of a large body of wispy white ectoplasm forming behind Jeff Taylor, seemingly reaching out for him.

Another creepy photograph from Big Woods is of Jeff's mother, Beverly Taylor; in it a large cloudy body of ectoplasm seems to be forming a face.

Because I investigate Big Woods Cemetery repeatedly, as does the Louisiana Spectral Research Center, the local sheriff's department is aware of our investigations. We always call them before we go to the cemetery and let them know when we will be arriving and about how long we plan to stay.

Many times a patrolman will drive by to chat with us. Some of them, too, have experienced things there themselves that they cannot explain.

One of the coolest paranormal manifestations in Big Woods Cemetery are the *fee fo lais*, as the Cajuns call them, also known as will-o'-wisps.

They are round balls of light, softball or grapefruit sized, that are seen bouncing along the gravel roads of the cemetery or spiraling down the pine trees. Many people, including me, have seen them in Big Woods. They are light green and seem to interact with us. Sometimes there will be only one; other times there will be two or three.

I have seen them in two locations in the cemetery. Occasionally they are seen near the site of the church, but mostly near the front of the cemetery along the gravel road that leads to the entrance, and in the trees and bushes to the north of that road.

One night I had a very close encounter with a *fee fo lais*. When we investigate a cemetery we park outside the gates if at all possible. Big Woods Cemetery Road is in the middle of nowhere and it dead ends at the cemetery. There are no houses along it.

That night cars kept driving up to the gate and then backing out, repeatedly. I was concerned about our automobiles, so when a car pulled back in again, I volunteered to sneak up and see what they were doing. I walked along the woods at the edge of the cemetery and then crossed to the other side of the gravel road, near the gate. The car backed out, and I walked onto the gravel road and started toward the gate.

When I was almost to the gate I just happened to look down; there was a *fee fo lais* not a foot from me, in an oleander bush. It was pale green and about the size of a large grapefruit. It was very bright. It startled me, and it disappeared almost as soon as I spotted it. It didn't frighten me, but it did make me jump from surprise.

I am not sure if *fee fo lais* are ghosts. I suppose it is possible that they are some sort of natural phenomena, such as swamp gas. However, they do seem to interact with us.

Interestingly, Beverly Taylor has photographed a very large bright green vortex in the area near the front of the cemetery where the *fee fo lais* are seen most often. It is the same green as the ball of light I saw. I have photographed the *fee fo lais*, and I hope to capture them on video next.

photo by Beverly Taylor

Tony and Natalie Lowery are members of the Louisiana Spectral Research Center, and good friends of mine. They specialize in recording electronic voice phenomena, or EVP. These are voices of the dead, or sounds such as cannon fire or horses galloping. They have investigated Big Woods Cemetery extensively, obtaining remarkable results.

Baseball hall of famer Ted Lyons is buried in Big Woods Cemetery, and one of the best EVPs Natalie and Tony have is from his grave. In it a voice says simply, "Play ball."

A gray apparition is seen in the back section of the cemetery, on the other side of the cattle guards from the main section. I have seen it more than once as it moves quickly among the trees.

Some of the members of the LSRC, including Beverly Taylor, Natalie and Tony Lowery, and Jamie Gates, had an amazing experience at the cemetery one night. They had walked through most of it and were coming back around near the site of the old church when they were engulfed in thick smoke. It was as if something large was burning, and they were having difficulty breathing.

They left the area as quickly as they could. After they caught their breath, they realized that they couldn't see the fire or smell the smoke from the gravel road. So they went back but could find no trace of the smoke or of anything that had been burning even though they had been choking in the thick smoke only a few minutes before.

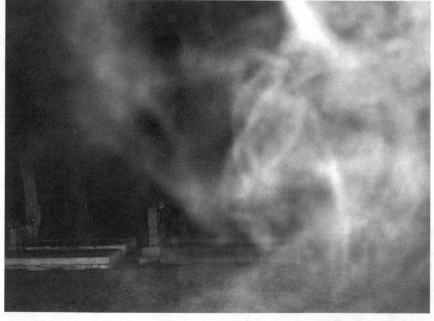

Big Woods is an amazing place that comes by its sinister reputation honestly. One night Natalie, Tony, and I were standing near the front of the cemetery photographing a hot spot. It was a clear night with a full moon. We were getting results, so we stayed there for a long time.

Then we noticed the fog. The air was clear and cool, but high in the trees, near the back section of the cemetery, a thin line of fog was advancing. We could see it in the bright light of the moon. We watched it move slowly along the back road, parallel to where we were standing. Then it started to wind its way through the trees toward us. It was fascinating, and we watched until it started to descend to our level, just in front of us. That was enough; Big Woods had made me leave, again.

Kate Fest and the Bell Witch

"I am a Spirit from everywhere, Heaven, Hell and the Earth;
I am in the air, in houses, any place at any time.
I've been created millions of years. That is all I will tell you."
—The Bell Witch

The Bell Witch stopped her attacks on the Bell family over a hundred years ago, but because of the violent and sensational nature of the haunting it still fascinates many today. Some say that old Kate Batts isn't quite done with Adams, Tennessee, and after my stay in Adams I am inclined to agree with them.

John Bell, his wife, Luce, and their nine children lived on a large plantation in rural Adams. John Bell was affluent and well respected by the community.

Well, respected by everyone except Old Kate Batts, that is. She and John didn't see eye to eye on many things, and some say that she was the type to hold a grudge. It was after her death that the Bell Witch first made her appearance, and indeed eventually the entity revealed itself as Kate Batts.

The haunting of the Bell family started in 1817 with the family noticing odd noises such as unexplainable scratching and flapping sounds coming from the outside of the Bell home.

The manifestations escalated into loud crashing noises as well as loud disembodied lip smacking and choking sounds. After a little over a year the haunting took a violent turn, pulling the hair of the Bell children as they tried to sleep. Soon the entity seemed to focus primarily on Elizabeth ("Betsy") Bell, who was twelve years old at the time.

The ghost tormented the child by pulling her hair, slapping her face, and eventually causing her to lose consciousness. Betsy's parents sent her to live with family friends, hoping that the ghost would not follow her out of the Bell house, but indeed it did, so Betsy returned home, where the phenomena continued to escalate.

The manifestations in the Bell home lasted for four years, and the house became famous. General Andrew Jackson is believed to have investigated the haunting, and it was reported on by several newspapers. Exorcisms were performed but failed, seeming only to make matters worse.

Many other cures were tried, including one in which Betsy drank a potion that caused her to have a "copious evacuation of the stomach." Sharp pins and needles were found in the vomit. On several occasions various members of the family found needles sticking out of cushioned chairs and pillows, with the sharp ends pointed out.

The haunting verbally manifested itself, first with whistling, then with a faint whisper, eventually becoming a loud booming voice that accused John Bell of drunkenness and child abuse. The entity embarrassed Betsy Bell in this manner to the point where the girl would break down into hysterics.

The witch went on to break up a romance between Betsy and Joshua Gardner, a local boy. "Please, Betsy Bell, don't have Joshua

101

Gardner. Please, Betsy Bell, don't marry Joshua Gardner," lamented the ghost in front of many witnesses.

Eventually John Bell became physically ill and was bedridden. The voice of the ghost continued to harass him, promising to do so until he was in the grave. One morning John wouldn't wake up, and an odd vial of black liquid was found in place of the medication prescribed by John's doctor. The witch proclaimed that she had poisoned John Bell, and indeed John died the following morning. The doctor tested the liquid on a cat, and the cat died almost immediately.

The witch then sang throughout John's funeral.

After John's funeral the witch proclaimed, "I am going, and will be gone for seven years." The ghostly manifestations stopped. Seven years later the ghost did return, but with only mild manifestations. After declaring that she would return in 107 years, she left again. 1935 came and went without incident, and so far Old Kate seems to have decided to maintain a low profile.

There are many theories concerning the Bell Witch, too many to go into here. The prevailing theory seems to be that the witch was a poltergeist, which is a German word meaning "noisy spirit." Poltergeists seem to center on children going through puberty, and Betsy Bell was the right age.

However, I think that while the Bell Witch haunting may have started out as a poltergeist, once the entity took on the identity of Kate Batts and ceased just being a "noisy ghost," it entered the realm of a malevolent haunting and I would no longer consider it to be a poltergeist. It has been my experience that poltergeists lack personalities. Of course, many people believe that several different entities are involved in the Bell Witch haunting, and that could be the case.

Another theory involves a cave on the Bell property that was used by the Bell family as a place to store perishables. Several years ago the grave of a Native American girl was found in the cave, and some believe that the Bell Witch was the product of a curse placed on the Bell property by the local Native Americans.

The Bell Witch haunting is so incredibly detailed that I suggest reading one of Pat Fitzhugh's books—*The Bell Witch; the Full Account* or *The Bell Witch*—or Troy Taylor's book *Season of the Witch* if you are interested in learning more about the history.

I've read about the Bell Witch many times over the years, so when Pat Fitzhugh, founder of the Bell Witch Historical Society and expert on the Bell Witch, asked me to speak at Kate Fest 2002, I was more than happy to do so. I invited my friend and fellow ghost hunter Mark Christoph to accompany me, and we were met there by two more friends, James Wardrop and Kalila Smith. Kalila was also speaking at Kate Fest.

Kate Fest is a conference/fair/seminar that pays homage to the Bell Witch and all her various incarnations. The 2002 event—the third one—was in October. It was held on the grounds of the old Bell School Building, appropriately because the school was built on what was once part of the Bell property. Also on the school grounds is an old cabin known as the Bell Log Cabin. It was built by the Bell family as a slave cabin, and later became a tenant farmer's house. In the late 1800s a second story and new floor were added to the cabin, and it is said that the wood used was from the infamous Bell home. This cabin would figure prominently in my Bell Witch experience.

In addition to my speaking duties, I was also to head a "mystery dare" event. There were a couple of them at this Kate Fest. Mine involved staying all night in the Bell Log Cabin. Kalila, a voodoo priestess, was to do a voodoo ritual/séance in the woods.

The voodoo ritual was held on the first night of Kate Fest. We took a hayride to a remote area surrounded by woods. A mill was located on the creek during the 1800s, and a girl was reportedly murdered in the creek there.

Kalila needed some assistance, so I drew some ritual symbols on the ground for her using incense. She gathered everyone into a circle around the symbols and had us hold hands while she spit out rum as an offering for the spirits and then joined hands with us in an attempt to communicate with them. Mark stood back by the tree line and took photographs.

After several minutes one of the participants felt something unseen push her; soon several others felt it too. One woman started to channel what she felt was the spirit of the murdered girl, and as she told us what she was feeling, she started to cry.

The girl seemed lost and confused, and Kalila tried to console the spirit and help her move on, but she seemed trapped.

Kalila has this to say about the séance:

"The séance I conducted at Kate Fest for the Bell Witch was one of my most frightening experiences. Several of us could hear the sound of "something" growling and circling us outside of the circle we had formed. I sensed the presence of a large wolf-like being hovering over me. This was no ghost, but something much stronger, and much more ominous. As we left, a thick rolling fog followed our path with what felt like a thousand eyes watching, waiting."

In the photographs taken by Mark during the séance, clouds of orbs appear to hover over the circle of people after Kalila joined hands with the rest of us.

The next night was my overnight stay in the Bell Cabin. Kalila and James had planned to stay all night with Mark and me, but the events of the night before had left Kalila drained and extremely tired. James wasn't feeling well either, so they both left the cabin early that night. About a dozen of us stayed.

Several of us had digital cameras, so we investigated the grounds of the school. After that, many of us were on the back porch of the small cabin when we noticed a thick fog coming in. The Bell Farm

photograph by Mark Christoph

property is separated from the school property by a barbed-wire fence, and the back porch of the cabin overlooks the property and a small pond. The fog came in very quickly from the direction of the Bell Farm, scaring a couple of people so badly that they went back inside the cabin.

Mark and I decided to walk down toward the barn area. The fog was really thick, and it was very dark. I heard a noise, and suddenly a large figure ran at me from the fog. I screamed a couple of expletives, and then realized it was Pat Fitzhugh. He had been waiting for me to get close enough so that he could scare me. We laughed for a few minutes, and then went back to the cabin, rounded up a few brave people, and headed for the Bell Cemetery.

Let me just say that this wasn't part of the itinerary. However, the cemetery was only a mile or so away, and that was too close for me to resist. The cemetery is locked after dark and has a high fence, so we walked along the front, taking lots of photographs, and then walked along one side. The air was clear; the fog seemed to be contained in the fields behind the cemetery. We were taking photographs of the graves by putting our cameras in between the bars on the fence. Mark was able to get a large vortex in one of his images with his digital camera.

photograph by Mark Christoph

We walked along the side of the cemetery, and in doing so we were well into the Bell Farm property. As we neared the end of the cemetery fence, we all noticed a dramatic temperature drop of about 30 degrees. The fog started to advance toward us from the field very quickly. We were all amazed at how fast it was moving; it was almost preternatural. Everyone wanted to leave, so we started back along the fence toward the road.

I started walking very slowly, but somehow I felt compelled to stay. I wanted to go into the field, toward the advancing fog, but Mark convinced me to continue with the others back to the cabin.

Some of the participants were asleep by the time we made it back. One man was sleeping so soundly that he was snoring. Pat Fitzhugh was asleep on the back porch. We decided to break out the Ouija board.

Now, I realize that Ouija boards are controversial, and I do not recommend their use to anyone. Communicating with the dead can be a risky thing to do, and you never know what you are going to attract when you use a Ouija board. It is like opening your front door and saying to whomever passes by, "Hey, come on in and stay with me for awhile." However, I am one of those "do as I say, not as I do" kinds of people, and I am okay with taking the risk myself. So, sometimes I use a Ouija board.

Another problem with Ouija boards is that you cannot trust any information you may get with one. Just because a being decides to talk to you doesn't mean it is going to tell the truth. On the contrary, it has been my experience that most of the information obtained with Ouija boards inevitably turns out to be either useless or downright hateful. It is almost as if the only ghosts willing to communicate that way are the spirits of mentally adolescent punks.

But we were stuck in a small cabin with a very creepy fog outside, so we decided to give it a shot. Mark Christoph hates Ouija boards, and I couldn't pass up an opportunity to freak him out. We lit some candles, and took turns placing our hands on the planchette.

Several people refused to participate, fearing the awesome power of the Bell Witch and not wanting to be implicated in whatever horrible events came to pass as a result of our using the Ouija board in the Bell Log Cabin. Minutes passed; nothing happened. We switched positions, thinking maybe our feng shui was off. Still nothing. It was most anticlimactic.

photograph by Mark Christoph

I decided to try another approach. I had recently learned how to do automatic writing. This is a technique for communicating with ghosts in which you allow the ghost to use your hand to write. I got a pad of blank paper and a felt tip marker and started to draw circles, which is a way to sort of loosen up. I remember starting to write that night, but not much after that. For some reason when I do automatic writing I remember very little of what happens; I am not sure why. My friends fill me in on what happened after I am done. Because I am not very mentally conscious during the writing, it is best if someone else asks questions out loud for the ghosts to answer.

The first person we contacted this way was Malcolm. Malcolm is a friend of mine; he and I were ghost-hunting partners when he was alive. He died tragically October 3, 2000, at the age of 36. Malcolm is usually who comes through when I try to automatic write. His writing style is very distinctive; he uses large letters and underlines his words.

Soon Malcolm was replaced by another ghost claiming to be "Bob Morrow." The writing style completely changed, with Bob's being much smaller and more precise than Malcolm's. Bob wrote the words "help, cold water, please" and pleaded "help my sister please."

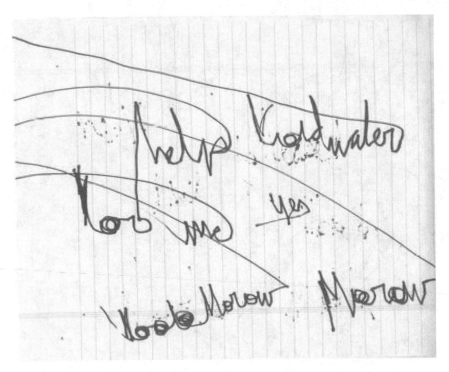

After a few minutes Bob was replaced by another entity that refused to identify itself. The handwriting changed once again, with this entity using big bold angular letters. It wrote "what do you want," "what do you want in my house," "mine," and "go away now." The entity seemed to get upset, and the words are much bigger and bolder as she (not sure why I want to say "she") asserted that we were to leave her house. Then she wrote "He will come" several times, along with "leave my house."

Then suddenly Bob was back for a very short time, saying only "it's ok" and "cold," along with "yes" to a couple of questions and writing his name "bob morrow."

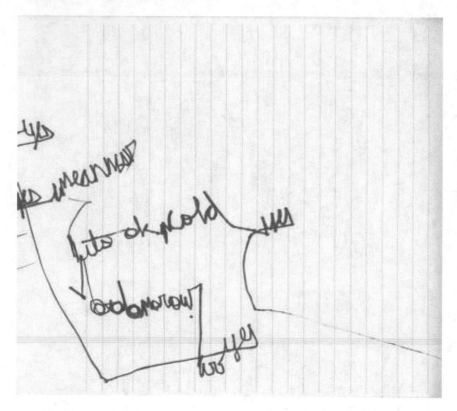

At this point I was very tired, and I stopped writing, unaware of what had transpired until later. Suddenly, as I leaned back from the papers, the guy who had been asleep and snoring the entire time leapt up and ran out the back door, violently vomiting on the porch and narrowly missing Pat Fitzhugh.

We were all shocked; the guy had been sound asleep just moments before. Throughout the night his wife had kicked him several times in an attempt to make him stop snoring, and it never fazed him. The guy and his wife left, but not before we asked them both if he had been drinking and if he was feeling ill. They both said no to both questions.

I am a professional paranormal investigator, but I have to say that as curious as I was, I still did not examine the vomit for pins and needles. I can say that I didn't hear anything hard drop to the floor during the episode.

We searched the Bell Family Cemetery the next day for Bob Morrow, and were unable to find a grave for him.

Had we been in contact with the Kate Batts? Did she make the sleeping guy vomit in an effort to make us leave? I don't know, but soon after that everyone decided to head back to their rooms.

I left Adams, Tennessee, with an uneasy feeling. I don't think the Bell Witch is done with Adams just yet, and I will be going back to see if I can figure out exactly what it is that she wants.

Kevin's House

Most paranormal investigators will tell you that ghosts can't hurt you. I will agree that usually they don't, but that doesn't mean they can't, and sometimes they do.

A couple of years ago I learned this lesson the hard way. I was involved in the investigation of an older home in Lake Charles, Louisiana, with the Louisiana Spectral Research Center. The owner of the home, Kevin, contacted the LSRC and requested an investigation. He wanted us to gather evidence in an effort to ascertain the identity of the ghost in his house.

The house is very normal looking and quaint, and Kevin has a decorator's touch. Each room is beautifully appointed, with special attention paid to the foyer and stairway. Kevin rents the suite of rooms upstairs out as an apartment, as well as a suite downstairs. He has lost several tenants due to ghostly shenanigans and wanted to find a way to appease the spirit.

We investigated the house several times, each time obtaining results that warranted more attention from us.

The house was built in the early 1900s by a dentist to house his family, including his wife, two children, and his sister. His office was in the front of the two-story house, and there are still bloodstains from his dental procedures on the hardwood floors.

The dentist died in the house after having a stroke that paralyzed half of his body. His sister died in the house soon after.

Early in the investigation we noted a column of energy in the foyer that we could not explain. We would get spikes consistently on our electromagnetic field detectors in a narrow area straight up from the bottom floor through the top floor.

Tony and Natalie Lowery are members of the LSRC who specialize in electronics, and they were able to map out a grid showing the exact dimensions of the column. One of the most interesting photographs I have is of this foyer. Paul Wing, another LSRC member, is holding an

EMF meter that is registering a redline spike, and just to the left and behind the meter is a small orb.

Natalie Lowery captured the image of an apparition on the stairs with her 35mm camera. It looks like a thin woman wearing a high-necked dress. There are strange things resembling lightning bolts surrounding the entity. Greg Stephens, another LSRC member, and I both captured an odd red and white anomaly on the stairs in photographs, on two separate occasions, with two different cameras. The manifestation in Greg's photo looks like it is reaching out to Beverly Taylor with two long tendrils, almost octopus-like.

photograph by Greg Stephens

We also photographed several vortices on the stairs.

During one of the earlier investigations of the house I was taking photographs with Beverly while Paul videotaped. After about 45 minutes I started talking to the ghost out loud while taking photos, and I made a few comments about how I thought the entity might be the ghost of the "spinster sister," who was supposed to have been a strict disciplinarian to her brother's children.

Just a few minutes later my left arm started to go numb, a sensation much like when a limb "falls asleep," all tingly. It was getting worse, and I told the others about it because it was really annoying me. After 15 minutes or so Beverly noticed that my arm was bleeding from two welts, one right under the other. There were raised horizontal marks on my upper arm, each with a thin line of blood where my skin had been broken. I did not feel the blows, and I did not bump into anything that would have caused them. It looked like I had been hit with a switch, twice.

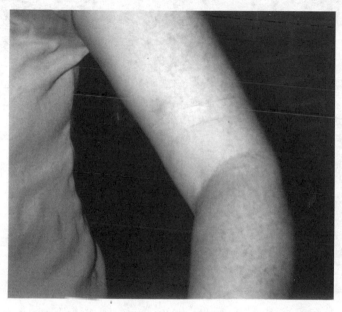

My arm stayed numb for almost an hour and was tingly for most of the night.

New Orleans

New Orleans is a dangerous city. Although murders happen on a daily basis, the press doesn't give much attention to crime, especially in the French Quarter; that would be bad for business. However, with a little effort you can find statistics about the murder rate in New Orleans—and it is appalling.

It is said that there are two or three serial killers in the French Quarter at any given time, and I believe it. So, from a ghost hunter's point of view, New Orleans is great.

New Orleans has been a bad place from the time of its very conception in 1718. The region has always been prone to excessive heat, annual floods, heavy rain, hurricanes, mosquitoes, and disease. Add to the mix a steady influx of disreputable settlers, usually given the option of going to prison or settling in New Orleans, and you have the makings of a very nasty place.

Lots of unhappy people, lots of violent crime, psychotics on every corner, a murderous martial history—what more could a ghost hunter ask for? I moved to the New Orleans area a little over three years ago.

New Orleans seems to draw negativity. Name a vice, and you are likely to find it flourishing in the French Quarter. Drugs, prostitution, gambling, and alcoholism contribute to the high suicide rate. Murders and suicides, obsessions, despair—these are the things ghosts are made of.

The occult swirls beneath the surface of the French Quarter. There are ritual drawings on walls, blue trim on doors and windows, and offerings of cigarettes, rum, and other less-savory items on sidewalks and in the city's many beautiful parks.

These are some of the more noticeable signs of voodoo, Santeria, and Satanism. The card readers and psychics have been moved to the sides of Jackson Square recently and forced to follow strict guidelines in an effort by officials to clean up the city, but the occultism cannot be banished that easily. It proliferates in the secret bars and hidden courtyards of the Quarter, and in the gated homes of the Garden District.

People ask me all the time where to find hauntings in New Orleans. I tell them that there are ghosts everywhere, especially in the French Quarter. However, some hauntings are more active than others. Below are accounts of three of my favorite hauntings, two of which I've investigated; the other one is simply too notorious to exclude.

photograph by Beverly Taylor

Julie

Julie, the ghost at the Bottom of the Cup Tearoom, is my favorite ghost. There is no historical evidence to back up the legends surrounding Julie, but she is one of the most active ghosts in the city.

According to legend, Julie lived at 732 Royal Street during the early 1800s. She was thought to be an octoroon, a person of mixed race—part black and part white.

The mixed race women of New Orleans were famous for their beauty, and wealthy white men would enter into domestic arrangements with these women, basically buying exclusive rights to them. This was known as *placage*, and it was very much a business deal, with the woman's family or former patron receiving a finder's fee and the woman receiving a house and maintenance for her and whatever children might result from the union.

Julie was part of such an arrangement. The house on Royal Street was part of her contract with a wealthy white man. Many of the men involved in placage relationships were already married, but this was not the case with Julie's lover. It is believed that the two of them were genuinely in love, and that love is what sealed Julie's doom.

Julie had all that she could want—a fine house, jewelry, beautiful clothes, slaves of her own, an exotic Persian cat—but still she wanted more. She wanted to be her lover's wife. He refused to marry her because in those days white men—especially wealthy white men—simply did not marry women of mixed blood.

The desire to marry the man she loved became an obsession with Julie, but no matter how much she pouted or begged, her lover refused to grant her wish. Finally, after yet another day filled with arguing over the subject, Julie's lover became exasperated and shouted to Julie, "Prove that you love me. Stay out all night on the roof, naked, and I will marry you." He thought she wouldn't do it. Julie was shocked at his suggestion, and he, believing that he had put an end to the subject of marriage, went out to dinner and an evening of cards with his friends.

That night a severe storm swept into New Orleans, as sometimes happens, and the temperature rapidly slipped below freezing. It was early morning, just before the sun came up, when Julie's lover arrived back home.

He went upstairs to the bedroom and was surprised to see that the bed was empty. He suddenly remembered his words from the night before. He rushed to the attic and looked out the small window to see a crumpled form near one of the chimneys. He climbed out onto the roof and found Julie, naked and huddled against the chimney in a vain attempt to keep warm. She was dead.

Her ghost has haunted the building ever since, and indeed is believed to have haunted her lover as well, because he died just a few months after Julie did.

Each winter, on the coldest night of the year, it is said that Julie can be seen, naked, dancing on the roof where she lost her life.

I have seen Julie, but she wasn't naked; she was wearing a long white frilly dress. A wedding dress maybe?

The building has three floors and an attic surrounding a small courtyard. There is a tiny pond of water in the courtyard with a stone cat in it; some say it is representative of Julie's beloved Persian. The ghost of a cat has been seen in the apartments. There is also an old wooden swing hanging from the balcony of what was once the slave housing and the kitchen.

The current owner of the building said that he took the swing down during remodeling. Immediately afterward he started having problems with tools missing and things breaking, and the usual ghostly manifestations seemed to increase in activity. While working on the stairs, he saw Julie standing on the stairs above him.

One of the psychics working in the tearoom casually mentioned that Julie was upset because her swing was missing. The owner put the swing back, the problems stopped, and he was able to continue remodeling.

My encounter with Julie was during a full night of investigation. The family who owns the building leases the upstairs apartments to various people. The man to whom they had leased the second-floor apartment had just moved out, so a local tour guide arranged to stay the night and investigate. She contacted me to photograph the investigation.

Five of us stayed in the apartment that night—my mother and I, the tour guide, a psychic, and a friend. We arrived after dark and unlocked the gate to the courtyard, locking it securely behind us.

We didn't know the history of the building; I prefer to investigate blind so that I am not influenced subconsciously by previous accounts. The tour guide set up a video camera, and I proceeded to take hundreds of photographs with my 35mm camera, some in black and white and some in color.

I photographed the apartment we were in, the courtyard, the winding staircase, and the little building on the side of the courtyard that housed the slaves and held the kitchen. That section was also three stories and is connected to the main building by a door at the end of the balcony on the upper floors.

It was during my initial wandering that I saw Julie. I had stepped out onto the landing of the stairs from the second-floor apartment. In front of me on the stairs was a woman wearing a long white ruffled dress. She had her back to me, and I could see that her black hair fell to a little below her shoulders. She ran down the stairs so quickly that in retrospect I know a human could not have moved that fast. I was startled, but took a photograph, perhaps a split second too late. There is no apparition in the photograph, but there is a white, human-sized shape on the stairs.

I was not scared; on the contrary, I was excited, and I ran down the stairs after her, trying to catch sight of her again, but I was not able to. I was so happy that I had seen her, and told the others about my sighting. The tour guide then told me that Julie has been seen in the courtyard and on the stairs wearing a white dress by many people.

After the initial excitement of this fantastic sighting wore off, we all settled down in the living room of the second-floor apartment. It was well past midnight. Some of us chatted, some dozed. All was calm for at least 30 minutes.

Suddenly the door to the landing slammed shut violently. Now, for those of you who haven't been to New Orleans, let me explain a thing or two about wind down here. It's either blowing really hard or not at all. Normally there is no wind, not even a slight breeze in New Orleans, and that night was no exception.

I stood up and walked over to the door and opened it. I didn't see anything. I took several photographs down the stairs and out over the courtyard. I turned and went back into the apartment, shutting the door behind me, and then I sat down on the floor next to the fireplace.

Right after I sat back down I felt what I can only describe as a wave of terror wash over me. I knew that something was at the door I had just closed, something horrible, and it wanted inside the apartment with us. I was terrified and unable to speak. The psychic burst into tears. Keep in mind I hadn't said a thing or indicated that anything was wrong.

I don't have words to tell you the dread that I felt. I had never experienced anything like it before, and I haven't again. I *knew* that something evil was leaning on the door frame, just outside, wanting in, wanting to hurt us. The violent emotion was overwhelming, and I am getting chills as I write about it now.

Suddenly it was gone, just as quickly as it had appeared. The psychic started talking about what she felt, and I confirmed everything she said. The entity was male, black, bald, a slave maybe. He was violent, murderous. He was wearing a white shirt that was unbuttoned. And his eyes—we both felt the intense hatred in his eyes, looking up at the door as he leaned on the frame. Neither of us had actually seen this entity, yet we'd both experienced the same thing.

After we calmed down, maybe an hour or so before the sun came up, we packed up our gear and left the building.

I was unable to sleep that morning, or for many nights after that. The encounter still haunted my dreams a year later.

The next day my mother and I went to lunch in the French Quarter. I didn't know the area very well then, and I didn't know the street names or how they ran in relation to each other.

After lunch my mother and I were walking back to our room. It was a warm, sunny day, and my attention was on the flagstones. I am a rock collector, and the slate sidewalks fascinated me. I was walking along, oblivious to my surroundings, when I stepped into a freezing cold spot of air. I stopped and asked my mom, "Why do I feel like I've stepped into a freezer?" We both looked around and then realized that I was standing in front of 732 Royal Street, and the Bottom of the Cup Tearoom.

That afternoon the tour guide called me. She said that they had watched the video from the night before. In it, just before the door slammed shut, you hear a woman's voice say, "Henri, *oeil rouge*." I didn't know what this meant, so she told me.

During the early 1800s most of the people in New Orleans spoke French. The Creoles had an expression, "*oeil rouge*," that they used to refer to someone they considered bad or evil. It means "red eye." We think the voice on the tape is Julie, and that she was warning us that "Henri red eye" was coming and shut the door to keep him out.

I wondered why I didn't see him or photograph him when I opened the door and stepped out onto the landing. Then it dawned on me that he had been coming up the slave staircase, which is just on the other side of the main staircase.

The tour guide told me that she'd heard accounts of Julie waking people up and saying what they thought was "are you John Rouge?" They guessed that John Rouge must have been her lover. We know now that she was speaking French, and that she wasn't asking for her dead lover. Instead, she has been trying to warn people about Henri for years.

This fit on many different levels. The building has a history of violence, and the man who vacated the apartment just before our investigation had undergone a dramatic personality change while living there. He was a medical student and was very social when he first moved into the building, playing cards and going to dinner with friends.

However, after being there a few months he started to become a recluse. He stopped going to class and then stopped going out completely. The only time his neighbors would see him was when they noticed him sitting in the back of the courtyard, in the dark, watching them. He did this for hours, on many nights. Sometimes he would sit on the balcony in the dark as well.

Eventually his parents grew concerned and came to New Orleans. They realized that something was seriously wrong with their son and took him back home.

I think that the negative energies from Henri oeil rouge had an impact on the man, and that it has affected many of the people who have lived in the building over the years. It certainly had a dramatic effect on me.

Initially, I wanted to go back the day we found all this out and started to put the pieces of the puzzle together. I was frightened but excited by what we had learned, and I wanted to know more. My mother, however, was less than enthusiastic. She took all the things that Julie had done and said as a warning, and it was obvious to her that Julie did not want us to go back there.

And the truth is, I have to admit I was relieved to have a reason not to face Henri. We left New Orleans that night.

When I developed my photographs from the investigation I was amazed at the results. I had phenomena in many of the images, including ectomist inside the apartment, an odd head-like anomaly on the balcony, an orb on the slave staircase, and many weird manifestations that I could not explain. Most surprisingly, however, was a photograph that my son's friend, Zack Menard, noticed a month after the pictures were developed.

The photograph is of the tour guide, the psychic, and her friend. They are in the bedroom of the second-floor apartment. I took the photograph from the large open area between the bedroom and the living room. In the image the tour guide's hair is being lifted up. She was totally unaware of it, as was I. It was as if someone was playfully

tugging a portion of it up. Also, in a mirror on the vanity against the wall is the image of a face that couldn't have been any of us.

It was over a year before I went back to the Bottom of the Cup Tearoom. This time I went with my ghost-hunting friends Malcolm Tillotson and Paul Wing. We met Kalila Smith at the tearoom. We then did a short investigation of the building once more. Kalila and Paul shot video, and Paul did audio recordings as well. Malcolm and I each focused on still photography.

Kalila was upstairs in the slave area when she started yelling excitedly to us. We ran upstairs to see tons of streaming orbs in her viewfinder. They were coming out of one little storeroom. Paul was able to capture them on video as well.

Then we noticed that the curtains on the door of one of the apartments were being moved as if someone were looking out at us, but no one was there. This happened for twenty minutes or so.

We got phenomena in our still photographs as well. Malcolm captured an amazing vortex of energy on the balcony of the slave quarters.

During the investigation Kalila and I talked to Julie as we went along, asking her questions. Paul Wing captured a woman's voice on his audio recording. It says "Je ne sais pas," which is French for "I don't know" or "I don't understand."

Since then I have visited the Bottom of the Cup Tearoom many times. The staff usually has new experiences with Julie to share. Most

photograph by Malcolm Tillotson

of the instances are benign and playful, like the time she slammed the balcony doors shut while the Discovery Channel was filming or the time she slid a heavy piece of glass across the counter.

However, occasionally something more disturbing will happen, like the time the owner's youngest son was working in the tearoom alone. The counter with the cash register was next to the far wall then, and as he leaned against it he kept feeling something hit his shoulder, like drops of water. However, he didn't see anything. This continued for several minutes before his sister returned and noticed a large dark red area on the back of his white shirt. It looked very much like blood to them both, but they could find nothing that he could have brushed against to result in that stain.

Nothing red was dripping from the ceiling, either. They were uncomfortable working in that area, and consequently the owner moved the counter to the other wall.

Julie is my favorite ghost, but despite her playful attitude, there is an undercurrent of something more sinister in the Bottom of the Cup Tearoom. Julie seems tied to the evil presence of Henri oeil rouge, and it makes me sad that I cannot free her.

The Jimani Lounge

The Jimani Lounge is located on the outer edge of the French Quarter, nearer to Canal Street than to the cathedral. This is the seedy, rough-and-tumble, urban side of the Quarter. Not much would shock or surprise the local denizens, mostly strippers who aren't glamorous enough to work on Bourbon Street, and drug dealers looking for a quick buck, but the events one Sunday evening in 1973 were an exception.

Reverend William Lawson, of the Metropolitan Community Church, had just finished his sermon in a back room of the Upstairs Lounge. This small bar was located in the rooms above the Jimani, and served a predominantly homosexual clientele. The Sunday evening services were attended heavily by the local gay community, and the bar was full.

Sixteen minutes later, twenty-nine people were dead; three more would die in the days that followed.

Just before 8 p.m., someone threw a Molotov cocktail into the narrow passage containing the stairs to the bar, igniting the entrance to the place. The fire grew unnoticed until someone in the Upstairs Lounge opened the door at the top of the stairs. The oxygen-starved flames rushed into the bar, engulfing the room. Many of the dead died instantly in this flash fire, but they were lucky in comparison to the people who couldn't escape.

Buddy Rasmussen, the bartender, acted quickly and managed to lead twenty people to safety over the rooftops. Sadly, not everyone was able to follow him.

The people who remained and were alive tried to escape through the windows, only to find that they were blocked by burglar bars. One man was small enough to squeeze through. The others, including Reverend Lawson, were caught half in and half out of the windows, and there they burned to death in front of a crowd of horrified onlookers.

Thirty-two people died in the fire, more than any other fire in New Orleans history. The arsonist was never identified.

One night many years later, Kalila Smith and I were having drinks at Pirates Alley Café in the French Quarter. She nonchalantly asked if I would like to check out a haunting with her, and then told me the sad history of the Jimani. The owner of the bar, Jimmy Massacci Jr., had called and asked that she investigate his place. I jumped at the chance, and we made plans to go.

Kalila, Jeff Taylor, and I arrived that first night after eleven. We started talking to Ronnie, the bartender, and he told us about the ghostly activity in the bar. The toilets in the women's bathroom would flush by themselves, and lights would go on and off.

More disturbingly, he told us that during the early morning hours when no one is in the bar, the employees would do work in the kitchen area. He said they would watch the bar at the same time, so they would only be in the kitchen for short periods of time.

On several instances the employees went into the kitchen, came back out, and found one of the television sets sitting on the floor. These sets are mounted in brackets near the ceiling.

Ronnie unlocked the door that led to what was once the Upstairs Lounge for us, after making it clear that he was too scared to actually enter the passage.

The minute he unlocked the doorway I could feel it, that feeling that something was very, very wrong here. We could still smell the smoke from the devastating fire in 1973. The stairs and the doors have been replaced, but the walls and ceiling still have scorch marks that are grim reminders of the blaze.

The three of us stepped inside as Ronnie waited on the sidewalk. I started snapping photos with my digital camera and I got phenomena right away. Kalila began to channel the spirits of the dead, and she was very uncomfortable. She said she could hear the screams of the victims and she could feel the fire. I have to admit, I felt warm myself.

I was excited by the results, so I made arrangements to go back. This time there were more of us—Kalila, Jeff, Johnny, Debe Branning, Rudy, and me. Jeff and Debe both shot infrared video. I took photographs with my digital again. Rudy and Kalila tried to communicate with the ghosts, but this time Kalila was affected by them so dramatically that she had to leave. She refuses to go back.

We were once again impressed by the results. Both Jeff and Debe captured phenomena on video. We decided to go back again, this time with a medium.

Melanie is a gifted medium from Los Angeles. She was a cast member from the USS *Hornet* episode of *Fear*. She came to visit me, and I lost no time in setting up another investigation at the Jimani. My friends James Wardrop, Cynthia Wade, and Jeff Taylor accompanied us.

The feeling hit Melanie on the sidewalk in front of the building. She started crying and said she could hear the screams. I hadn't told her the history of the place, or even where we were going. We waited outside for a while to let her calm down, and then proceeded to the passage. I was shooting video in infrared this time and Jeff was using the digital camera.

I could see phenomena immediately in my viewfinder and Jeff started getting it in the still images as well. Melanie began to channel so intensely that she had to sit on the stairs to keep from falling. She said that the spirits were trying to flee and her legs were shaking violently. James has his own methods of communicating with the dead, so he went to the top of the stairs and crouched quietly. I stayed on the landing in the center of the stairs and recorded everything.

photograph by Jeff Taylor

Melanie continued to channel and the ghosts started trying to speak through her. She kept repeating the words "Keri, Keri care, care Karen Carol," but she couldn't understand what the ghost was trying to say. She felt compelled to move to the top of the stairs, so I helped her climb up. She calmed down once she made it to the top landing, only trembling intermittently.

I film with my right hand holding the video camera up and my left hand down. That night I could feel heat on my left hand, and then it switched to my right and started to intensify to the point where it was almost unbearable. My throat began to constrict and it became harder for me to breathe. All this time I was getting orbs streaking all over the narrow passage on video. It took all my effort to continue filming and ignore the sensations I was feeling.

photograph by Jeff Taylor

Finally Melanie had to leave, and I took that as my cue to stop filming.

The video footage from that night is amazing. When Melanie started channeling, her whole body language changed dramatically. The orbs streak by in clusters, extremely fast, some seeming to originate from the hole in the ceiling caused by the fire. Unlike dust, these anomalies moved quickly, without benefit of air currents.

I researched the deceased from the fire. One was named "Clarence." Could that have been the ghost Melanie was channeling? Or was the entity making a reference to a loved one it would never see again? Or maybe one of the murdered souls knows who committed this horrible act of arson and is determined to seek justice.

—————⌒—————

The Lalaurie House

The most famous haunting in the French Quarter is that of the Lalaurie House, at 1140 Royal Street. Unlike Julie and the Bottom of the Cup Tearoom, the horrible history of the Lalaurie building is easily verifiable through newspaper accounts and other records from that time. The large gray building, which takes up most of a city block, was built in 1832 by Dr. Louis and Madame Delphine Lalaurie.

Delphine was known for her cruelty, and local authorities took the unusual action of taking her slaves away after she was seen by neighbors chasing a slave girl with a whip. The terrified girl leapt from the second story of the house to her death on the street below.

However, the unfortunate slaves were later returned to Delphine by her family, who secretly bought the slaves as they were auctioned.

In 1834 the house on Royal Street caught on fire while Dr. Lalaurie and Delphine were having a dinner party. The guests watched from a safe distance as firemen put out the fire. Oddly enough the fire had been deliberately set by a slave who was found chained to the large woodstove.

While checking each room in the house, the firemen found a room in the attic that was barred and locked. They broke down the door and were horrified by what they saw inside.

Over a dozen slaves were in the small attic room. Some were chained to the walls, some were in cages, and many were dead. Strapped to an operating table was a slave who appeared to be the victim of an attempt at a sex change operation. It was obvious from the condition of the slaves and from the buckets of human organs and limbs that slaves had been used for medical experimentation and torture.

Those slaves who were still alive were rushed to the local hospital, and a few actually survived. Two went to work for the Barnum & Bailey Circus. One woman who had had her limbs broken and reset at odd angles by the Lalauries was known as the Crab Lady. Another was the Caterpillar Lady; she'd had her skin removed in strips down her body.

Word of the atrocities spread quickly through the French Quarter that night, and a mob soon surrounded the Lalaurie house. The Lalaurie family managed to escape in their carriage and were never seen in New Orleans again.

Some say the family moved farther north to a plantation on the Mississippi, some say the family moved to Europe. In the 1940s a small plaque was found in St. Louis 1 Cemetery on alley 4 bearing the name "Madame Delphine Lalaurie."

Had she secretly returned?

The ruins of the house were deserted for several years. Locals refused to walk on the sidewalk near the house because they feared the ghosts that could be heard screaming from the burned walls.

After a few years, however, crowding in the city made it impossible to ignore the large building on the corner of Royal Street, so the house was rebuilt and used as a girls' school and then a tenement apartment before being turned again into a private home.

Over the years since the Lalauries owned the place, several people have died in the house—at least one, Edoard Vigne, under mysterious circumstances. He lived alone, and was found dead in his apartment after black crepe, a local custom signifying a death in the family, was noticed decorating the door.

Many ghostly manifestations were reported during the tenement years. One woman woke to see the apparition of a dark-haired woman leaning over her baby's bed, smothering the infant with a pillow. The ghost of a naked black man in chains was seen walking down the stairs by several startled tenants.

The building at 1140 Royal Street has been used by the Freemasons, the bottom turned into a bar and billed as "The Haunted Saloon," and was even briefly used as a furniture store. The furniture store did not last long. The merchandise was ruined several times, found mysteriously covered with a foul liquid filth by the owner.

More recently, the house was owned by a physician, Dr. Albright. He refused to discuss the hauntings. He sold the building to Dr. Moss, another physician. Both refused investigations of the building.

I have not been inside the Lalaurie house, but I have hundreds of photographs of the outside. The front door is a paranormal hot spot, and I have still photographs of many different anomalies in this area, including vortices, orbs, and an actual apparition of what looks like a servant boy.

I have photographed ectomist several times on the balcony that runs along the upper portion of the building.

The tortured souls of slaves do haunt 1140 Royal Street.

As for the spirit of Madame Delphine Lalaurie, I cannot say for sure. However, I do not doubt that her malevolence could continue after death, and it wouldn't surprise me to find that her evil presence remains to endlessly torment the helpless slaves she brutalized in life, as well as the living.

Lafayette Vampire

Do you believe in vampires? I would have laughed a few years ago if someone had asked me this question, but not now, not after an encounter I had in an old Catholic cemetery in Lafayette, Louisiana.

Things started, appropriately enough, in New Orleans, in a bar in the French Quarter. My boyfriend, James, and I were having drinks and talking about vampires. The bartender leaned over to us and said, "I know where you can find a real vampire, but you can't just waltz into the place; there are things you have to do first if you want to see it."

Something about the man seemed not only sincere but completely serious. We were hooked. After a few hours of talking over the pros and cons, he gave us a set of detailed instructions and directions to the cemetery in Lafayette.

According to the bartender, we had to make ourselves more vampire-like in order for the vampire to show itself to us.

Then we were to hang out in the cemetery at night, become familiar to the environment, and allow the entity to observe us. We would spend a couple of hours a night, two or three nights a week, in there.

The cemetery was not completely fenced in back then, and we were able to walk around the aboveground tombs and play in the giant oak without fear of being arrested.

We did this for most of the summer, through the fall, and into winter. We didn't see anything unusual, and the cemetery was almost preternaturally, well, dead. Nothing out of the ordinary happened during all those months.

Then, one night just before Christmas, we decided to go to the cemetery again. A cousin from out of state and James' best friend came with us. When we arrived I decided to walk to the front near the cathedral by myself because I didn't think I would see anything if a group of people came with me. They all went toward the back.

The next thing I remember is the realization that I was running through the cemetery. It is an old Catholic cemetery and most of the tombs are above ground and not regularly spaced. It is an erratic mix of large tombs, headstones, and family crypts, scattered without order, and I was running as fast as I could through them.

Then I realized that I was chasing something.

It was moving ahead of me. All I remember is a dark shape and the swinging of something behind it, like loose fabric. I followed it through the center of the cemetery, directly behind the cathedral, and then off to the left toward the tree line that went along the high hurricane fence.

When it reached the trees, it stopped and so did I. It turned to look at me, and all I could make out was a white oval of a face in the darkness. I could see no features. Then it was gone.

I immediately sank down onto an aboveground tomb. I was exhausted and had no energy left at all. A few minutes later James and the others walked up. They immediately noticed that something was wrong, and I told them that I had seen something very strange.

Then suddenly we all smelled garlic. It was overwhelming, as if someone were cooking a pot of spaghetti sauce right under our noses, but this was in the middle of a cemetery, in the middle of the night.

Up until this point I was not afraid, but for some reason the garlic smell made me want to leave, so we did. Looking back, I realize that I was not thinking clearly, my mind was befuddled by what I had encountered.

The next day I received a phone call from my mother. She asked what I had done the night before. I said nothing much. Then she told me about a dream that she had had. In the dream I was walking in a creek, and as I walked I was stirring up mud and something evil was following the mud back up the stream to meet me. I cracked and told her everything.

We both agreed that my vampire hunts would cease, and that the events of the night before were a warning. I haven't been back inside that cemetery at night.

Did I encounter a real vampire, or was it just a ghost with delusions of grandeur? If it was, indeed, a vampire, why did it show itself to me and then allow me to leave alive? Was it what is known as a psychic vampire, sucking the energy from my body rather than the normal vampire diet of blood?

Even now I look for the bartender when I am in the French Quarter. I didn't get his name, and no one seems to remember him. Maybe he has the answers.

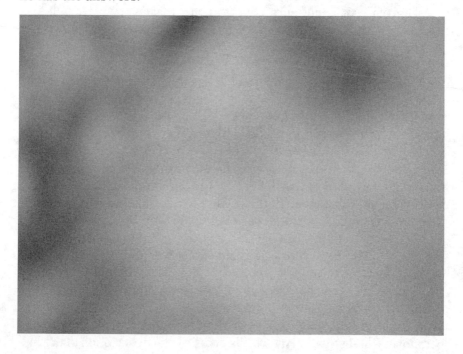

Battlefield Ghosts

Battlefields are among the most haunted of locations. The sudden death, anguish, confusion, suffering, and guilt felt by the soldiers is more than enough to bring about the disturbed state of mind necessary for the soul of the deceased to remain after the body has died.

Therefore, it is not surprising to learn that every battlefield has tales of ghosts, and indeed every battlefield I have investigated has proven to be haunted.

It seems to me that battlefields, more than graveyards, are somber places, enveloped in the sadness of lives cut short and the pain felt by men embroiled in disputes that many times weren't of their own making. I investigate battlefields with an almost hallowed reverence, conscious of the sacrifices made by the soldiers and determined to do my best not to disturb them.

The town of Gettysburg and the surrounding area is by far the most famous haunted battlefield in the United States. More men fought and died during the Battle of Gettysburg than in any other battle on American soil. The battle was eventually won by the Union Army after three days of intense fighting and over 51,000 casualties. Additionally, 5,000 horses were killed, and one of the most active hauntings in the area involves a horse.

Sachs Bridge is a covered bridge that was built in 1852. During the Battle of Gettysburg the Confederate Army retreated across this bridge, leaving many of their dead along the way. Local historian and paranormal investigator Andy Mills gives a brief description of the history of Sachs Bridge:

"Located about one mile behind Warfield's Ridge, the main Confederate line of battle on July 2, Sachs Bridge witnessed much during the few days of the battle: from the Confederate advance preceding the battle to the remnants of the Southern Army retreating a few days later. Sachs Bridge itself and the surrounding fields would bear witness first-hand to the destruction wrought upon the Gettysburg area: from Rebel

deserters who were hung from her rafters to the unmarked mass graves in the surrounding fields. Sachs Bridge is truly a haunted location...

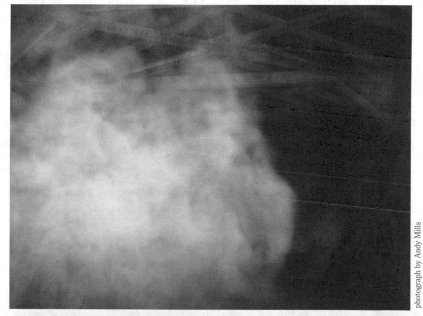

photograph by Andy Mills

photograph by Andy Mills

The photographs taken by Andy Mills and his wife, Kim, are among the best ghost photographs I have seen, and are the very best from the Gettysburg area. One photograph in particular, from Sachs Bridge, shows the apparition of a horse with a rider appearing in a cloud of ecto. It is an amazing photograph, as is the one taken just afterward, when Andy and his wife were making their own retreat from the bridge.

In it, the apparition of a horse is even more evident. Andy recalls that night:

"The night of October 13, friends of ours decided to head to Gettysburg for a night out. After spending time on the battle-field, we decided to head to the bridge to see what might lurk in the darkness. At the time, we were not seasoned ghost hunters. Although we had some exciting experiences, we were not heavily into the picture aspect of ghost hunting. Upon arriving in the little parking lot adjacent to the bridge, the four of us walked over to the opening of the bridge, and I snapped a picture.

Having never seen ectoplasm before, I was curious as to why I couldn't see much out of the viewfinder. Our friend immediately brought to our attention that he noticed something prevented the flash from projecting outward, almost like part of the light from the flash hit a brick wall and didn't continue past it. Having used a digital camera, we immediately checked out the picture and noticed it was nothing like we have seen before.

If you look carefully you can make out a horse and a rider on it. Some people even go so far as to say they see another face or two in the rafters. In the bottom-right corner of the ecto-plasm, the whiteness turns to a brownish color (the only time I have ever witnessed this phenomena), which is the tip of the horse's nose.

A little further up, you can see the harness over the horse's nose. Following the brownish ectoplasm further up, you can see the horse's eyes, as well as its mane. Sitting in the center of the picture is the face of its rider, staring directly at the viewer."

Someday soon I plan on joining Andy and Kim Mills on a late-night visit to Sachs Bridge and to the other hauntings of Gettysburg.

I have investigated many battlefields over the years and they were all haunted, but my experiences at three of them make those three stand out: Stones River, the Battle of Buzzard's Prairie, and Chickamauga.

The Battle of Stones River and Hell's Half Acre

THE VETERANS OF SHILOH HAVE LEFT A DEATHLESS HERITAGE OF FAME UPON THE FIELD OF STONE RIVER
—Hazen Brigade Monument

The Battle of Stones River, near Murfreesboro, Tennessee, was one of the bloodiest of the Civil War. The fierce fighting took place from December 31, 1862, through January 2, 1863. The South eventually won the battle, but the price was high. The Confederates lost 11,739 lives, and the Union lost 12,906. Many of the Confederates died trying to take Hazen's Brigade and Hell's Half Acre.

The Round Forest area near Stones River was renamed Hell's Half Acre by the Confederate soldiers embroiled in a fierce battle with Hazen's Brigade. The nine acres, really just a clump of scrubby cedars, was the site of numerous infantry charges into Union commander William B. Hazen's troops who had a protected position on the ridge overlooking the area. Hazen's Brigade was the only Union position able to hold its ground throughout the first day of battle.

The Confederates soldiers were forced to make their charges in the open where they were mowed down by Union artillery and gunfire. Several Southern brigades were thrown into battle against the Union position, only to be repelled by the devastating firepower of the Union soldiers. The 8th Tennessee lost 306 men out of 425. The 16th lost 207 out of 402. One Federal soldier said that the Confederates must have believed they had "opened the door of Hell, and the Devil himself was there to greet them."

A contemporary account gives an apt description of the horrible aftermath of that day's assault:

> *Cold rain fell in the darkness on thousands of dead and wounded strewn over the landscape. The wounded cried out for help, for water, for a fire, to God or for their mothers, or simply to be shot and put out of their pain. Attending to them was such a task that most of the dead could only be left where they had fallen, their blood freezing to the ground.*

The following day saw Hazen's position as the only remaining Federal defensive line at Stones River. On January 2 Confederate Major General John C. Breckenridge was ordered to take the high ground beyond Hell's Half Acre from Hazen.

Breckenridge firmly objected, believing the task to be impossible, but was overruled by his superiors. He attacked with 4,500 men, and was driven back. He lost 1,700 soldiers in the attack.

The Union Army had kept the hill, but at a terrible price. Fifty-five of Hazen's men are still buried on that hill today, surrounding the first monument of the Civil War.

On it is written:

THE VETERANS OF SHILOH HAVE LEFT A DEATHLESS HERITAGE OF FAME UPON THE FIELD OF STONE RIVER.

THE BLOOD OF ONE THIRD ITS SOLDIERS TWICE SPILLED IN TENNESSEE CRIMSONS THE BATTLE FLAG OF

THE BRIGADE AND INSPIRES TO GREATER DEEDS: ERECTED 1863 UPON THE GROUND WHERE THEY FELL.

Many of the surviving men on both sides of the conflict would meet again soon, at Chickamauga.

Mark Christoph and I arrived in Murfreesboro in early October, just before sunset. Neither of us knew the history of the battle of Stones River at the time, but we did know that it was a battlefield and that battlefields are haunted, so that was enough to catch our interest.

We spotted a large monument on a hill and decided that would be a good place to start our investigation. There was a scrubby patch of small trees to one side and an open area with a few large trees directly in front of the hill.

We both took photographs with our digital cameras as we explored the hill and the area inside the stone wall surrounding the monument. We both started to capture faint phenomena in our photographs.

My attention was drawn to the wooded area, so I walked over to it. The thick cedar trees weren't very tall, but paths had been worn among them, and the floor was coated with soft needles from the trees. I hadn't gone very far when I got a bright orb in one of my photos. I took several shots, and the orb stayed in the general area.

I decided to try to communicate with the ghost. I started to talk to the ghost of what I assumed was a soldier. I continued to take photographs intermittently; the ghost did not seem to be afraid of the camera flash, as is sometimes the case.

I could see in the images that the orb was moving closer, so I held out my hand. Amazingly, in one of the next shots the orb was just a couple of feet from my outstretched hand. It had responded to my voice and my gesture. Then it was gone, no longer appearing in the following shots.

I was excited, and went to tell Mark. He had been getting pronounced phenomena on the hill, especially near two graves that are located outside the stone wall.

We decided to explore the wooded area together. We followed a winding path through the cedar trees, occasionally getting faint phenomena in our photographs. The sun was completely down now, and it was dark, but we could still see enough to make our way down the path.

Suddenly, something hit the right side of my face. It felt like a hand, but I knew Mark hadn't slapped me; indeed, he was several feet in front of me. I looked around for a branch or something that I could have run into, but I was in a small opening near a large tree, and there was nothing around that could explain the blow.

I continued through the woods behind Mark. Soon the right side of my face began to burn. The feeling intensified to the point where it was extremely uncomfortable. Mark examined my face with the flashlight, but he didn't see any physical indication of the pain, not even a reddened area. I was surprised because the sensation I felt was almost unbearable.

We made it to the other end of the wooded area and crossed a wooden fence. My face started to feel better. We walked along the railroad tracks until we reached a large cemetery with a stone wall. I climbed onto the top of the wall and sat down to rest. The burning on my face was rapidly dissipating, but was still bothering me. Mark climbed the wall and jumped down into the cemetery to do a brief camera sweep.

By the time he returned, my face felt fine. He didn't get much phenomena in the cemetery, and it was late, so we decided to walk back to the truck.

As soon as we climbed back over the fence into what I now know was Hell's Half Acre, the right side of my face started to burn again. This time the pain was much worse, and it was all I could do to just follow Mark down the path. It felt as if one side of my face was literally on fire.

We eventually made it back to the monument. Once again, as soon as I exited the wooded area my face started to feel better, although it remained tender for a longer period this time than it had before. We left Stones River.

I cannot explain what happened to me that night. Had I tapped into the suffering still felt by the spirit of a dead soldier?

Or had one of the ghosts felt that I was somehow irreverent in my approach and decided to teach me a lesson?

Chickamauga

"We can die but once, this is the time and the place!"
—Brigadier General William H. Lytle

Many Civil War historians consider the battle of Chickamauga to be the most tragic of the conflict. Over 34,000 men died during the two days of engagement on September 19 and 20, 1863.

During that first day of battle it was apparent to both the soldiers and their commanders that this was not an ideal place to fight. The thick forests made traditional fighting methods impossible, and cannons were useless, except in the occasional open field. There were no clear-cut battle lines, and the soldiers had to resort to hand-to-hand combat.

Soon the ground was soaked in blood as wave after wave of men were thrown into battle. The dead and wounded were stacked like cordwood to make way for the advancing soldiers.

The weather turned bitterly cold, and the fighting ended when the sun went down. However, the temporary ceasefire had a horrible side effect. The quiet after the din of battle meant that the piteous cries of the thousands of dying and wounded men could be heard throughout the night. Any attempt to enter the fields by either side was met with gunfire, so nothing could be done to help the wounded.

The second day saw the Union lines crack under the fury of the Confederate attack. The remaining Union forces made a desperate stand in the woods and fields of Snodgrass Hill. The Snodgrass family was forced to flee into a ravine as the battle consumed the land around their cabin. The cabin soon became a makeshift field hospital as the bloodiest fighting of the battle waged just outside its doors.

Union General Thomas held Snodgrass Hill throughout several charges by the Confederates, though his men were running short on ammunition, earning himself the nickname "The Rock of Chickamauga." The Union soldiers resorted to using bayonets to fight off the flood of thousands of Confederates.

That night they evacuated, leaving behind many of the grievously wounded. Union General Beatty described the retreat:

"The march to Rossville was a melancholy one. All along the road, for miles, wounded men were lying. They had crawled or hobbled slowly away from the fury of the battle, become exhausted, and lain down by the roadside to die."

The Confederate Army won the battle of Chickamauga.

My friend Mark and I arrived in Chattanooga, Tennessee, on the anniversary of the bloody Civil War battle at Chickamauga. We decided to investigate the battlefield that night.

It rained most of that day, but it had stopped by the time we entered the battlefield. It was really foggy, so any ghost photography would have been unreliable; however, we both wanted to explore the area.

We drove through the park, noting the many small monuments and stacks of cannon balls. The area is very isolated from the surrounding suburbs; it is mostly forest intermingled with some open fields.

We turned down a little side road and drove through a field and then some thick woods. It was very dark in this section of the battlefield, with no streetlights or buildings. We spotted an open field surrounded by woods. There was a hill at the back and a large monument. We decided to hike up to it and take some photographs.

The fog was starting to thicken in the field as we walked along the tree line. We found a small trail to the right cutting through the woods. It was very dark and creepy, so of course we walked down it.

After some time we decided to turn back and continue up the hill. We started walking toward the field when suddenly we heard a loud stomping noise, like a big horse stomping on dry earth.

The ground was extremely muddy. The sound it made was a very heavy thud, and it seemed to be just inside the trees but out of our sight. We were startled but intrigued. Mark continued down the path a little way, hoping to hear the sound again, and I stood under a tree to reload my camera. Just as I had the back of my camera open, something shook the tree I was standing under so hard that I was showered in water droplets. I jumped out from under it and quickly loaded my camera. I took several photographs of the tree but nothing unusual was in the images.

Mark met me at the edge of the field and then we both continued up to the hill and the monument. He said that he had heard the stomping noise once more while he was alone.

We explored the area surrounding the hill and the cleared part of the hill itself. Then Mark noticed a tiny path through the dense woods behind the monument. It was very creepy, with the fog and the dark forest surrounding it, and the canopy of trees completely shut out what little moonlight there was.

We started down the path and made it to a tiny clearing with a couple of cannons. Suddenly we heard the stomping noise again and a sharp rapping sound very close, like something was hitting a piece of wood against a tree. We were surprised and confused. The woods were very dense and if an animal or even a human had been following us, surely we would have heard them as they made their way through the underbrush.

We decided to focus on the cleared section of the hill and leave the wooded area.

We walked back to the hill and watched as patches of fog shifted from one area to the other. We both heard a loud report that sounded just like a gunshot. Then a few minutes later we heard what sounded to us like cannon fire. We knew that re-enactors would be camped out for the anniversary, but we didn't think they would be firing weaponry that late at night, as it was after midnight by this time.

It started to rain again, so we reluctantly left, deciding that we would come back again the following night.

As we made our way back to the truck we heard the rapping noise again, followed by the stomping sound, this time at the bottom of the hill. It seemed to be just inside the tree line again.

The next day we visited the battlefield museum, then went to a bookstore after dinner. While looking through a couple of books on the area I came across the legend of Old Green Eyes.

According to several books on local lore, a large, hairy creature with glowing green eyes haunts the woods of Snodgrass Hill. It was seen on the battlefield the night of the first battle, roaming among the dead and wounded men. Native American accounts have told of a similar Bigfoot-like creature inhabiting the area for many years before that.

Old Green Eyes has been seen repeatedly in the years following the Civil War. At least one car wreck occurred near Snodgrass Hill when someone became hysterical after seeing the creature.

Park employees have seen it as well. Roger Tinney, a former park ranger, admits that he saw the creature walk across the road in front of him one foggy night. It paused to look at him, and he was transfixed by its green eyes, which slowly faded into the thick fog.

It didn't take Mark and me long to realize that the hill we had been on the night before was Snodgrass Hill. Also, we found out that the most intense fighting was on the ridge behind the monument but through the woods. That night was the anniversary of the engagement. In other words, that night was perfect for ghost hunting in the woods of Snodgrass Hill.

This revelation disturbed me. The one thing that I was extremely afraid of at the time was Bigfoot. I've had nightmares about being chased by Bigfoot for decades. In them it is night, and I am running through a thickly wooded area in heavy fog. I can hear the creature as it closes in behind me, and just as its hairy arm is reaching out for me I wake up. Of course, the woods in my dream looked just like the woods we had been in the night before in Chickamauga.

I admit I was scared, but I was determined to go back.

It was dark when we drove back to Snodgrass Hill. The fog was just starting to roll in. I sat in the truck and looked at the woods, and after I whined for a few minutes, I got up my courage, and Mark and I walked up the hill.

I could handle ghosts, but Bigfoot freaked me out. I whined some more on the way, and Mark assured me that Bigfoot had never killed anyone and that we would be fine.

I stared at the dark, foggy trail behind the monument. I was more scared that night than I had been in a long time. When I get scared I get mad, so finally I just started walking, quickly, down the path. Mark started taking photographs as we went. We walked for more than a mile through the woods, accompanied by my constant stream of profanity. We reached the end of the trail and it split three ways.

I asked Mark which way we needed to go. I didn't want to stand still for long because I was scared and I just knew that Old Green Eyes was watching us from behind one of the trees. Mark wasn't sure which way to go; he thought we should go up a couple of steps onto a trail that went even deeper into the woods. But he wasn't certain.

That was where I drew the line. There was no way that I was going to continue to walk through those woods when we didn't even know for sure which way the ridge was. I talked Mark into walking back to the truck with me, ostensibly to get the park map so that we would know which path to take.

The walk back through the woods was even worse. The fog was getting thicker by the minute, and I kept waiting to hear the stomping noise or see a big dark shape step out onto the trail in front of us.

We made it back to the truck and looked at the map. Mark was right; the ridge was up the steps. However, by that time I had given up. I didn't have a gun or even a pocketknife. I couldn't go back into those woods again.

Since then I have gotten over my fear of Bigfoot, for the most part, and I am actively hunting for one. However, when I think about those woods and the heavy fog, I get chills. I know I am going to have to go back some day and face Old Green Eyes.

———————❧———————

The Battle of Buzzard's Prairie

"The fight was a desperate one for several hours, my own
regiment losing nearly forty percent of its strength in killed
and wounded – but it ended in defeat of the immediate
Federal force, the capture of the camp and its many guns,
and nearly a thousand prisoners. I had five color bearers
shot dead in the battle, the eyes of the sixth one shot out,
but my colors never struck the ground."
—Colonel Wilbur H. King

The battle of Buzzard's Prairie was a small skirmish in comparison to
the major engagements of Stones River and Chickamauga. However,
the dead are not concerned with such comparisons and this small battlefield is one of the most active that I've investigated.

The battle took place on the land of Chrétien Point Plantation and
on the banks of Bayou Bourbeau, near Sunset, Louisiana.

The plantation house itself was spared only because the owner at
the time, Hypolyte Chrétien III, signaled the advancing Federal troops

by making the Masonic sign from the upper gallery of the house. The Union commander was a Mason, and he allowed the building to remain standing.

At one point during the battle the house was caught in the crossfire between Confederate troops entrenched along the bayou and Union troops on the plantation grounds. The building was struck by cannon and rifle fire, and some of the bullet marks can still be seen on the outside doors and walls.

The battle took place November 2 and 3, 1863. I investigated the battlefield on the anniversary with a group of ghost hunters, including Tony and Natalie Lowery, Greg Stephens, and my psychic friend, Rebecca.

We investigated the plantation house first. The ghosts of Felicite Chrétien and a pirate, whom she shot on the stairs, are known to roam the structure. The pirate's body was placed in a small room under the stairs and kept there until the local authorities arrived a few days later. The bloodstains remain on the stairs.

It was late at night by the time we made it out onto the battlefield.

Sugarcane is grown on the site of the battle, but it had been harvested a few weeks before our investigation.

It had rained all day, and the field was extremely wet and muddy. The plantation and battlefield are miles from town, and isolated from neighbors.

We made our way into the muddy field from the road, photographing as we went along. Tony Lowery was recording audio. He uses a parabolic ear, which is a very sensitive device used to record the slightest sound. We had been in the field for about 20 minutes when we all heard what sounded like a bugle call. It was only four notes, and it was not a melody any of us recognized. A few minutes later we all heard the sharp report of gunfire.

Natalie Lowery was wearing her electromagnetic field detector in a net pouch hanging from her coat. This particular model had small lights that indicate the presence of an electromagnetic field. The lights range from green to red, red indicating a strong electromagnetic signal.

I noticed that her meter was pegged at red, so I took a photograph. As I did we all heard what sounded like a horse galloping on hard earth. When my camera flash went off I saw a large brown object directly in front of us that moved quickly to the left. The object appeared to be about four feet off the ground. It disappeared even though there was no place for it to hide in the large open field.

We continued to the back of the field, but nothing else unusual happened. After a while we decided to get back into our cars and drive down to Marland's Bridge.

Marland's Bridge is a small bridge over Bayou Bourbeau. During the Civil War the Confederates occupied the bridge. A group of Union soldiers was isolated on the other side from the main body of Union troops. In a desperate bid to escape, Lieutenant Marland loaded his soldiers onto a wagon and stormed the bridge.

He managed to get through, although several of his men were killed in the attempt. He was awarded a medal for his courage, and the bridge has been known as Marland's Bridge since.

Another incident happened on Bayou Bourbeau during the Civil War. A cousin of the Chrétiens was staying with the family while the men were off fighting for the Confederacy. When the men were able to

visit their families they would take a boat down the bayou to the plantation landing.

The cousin became despondent after her husband had not come home for many months. She began to take her small son and walk down to the landing to search for her husband. She also went there late at night, so the family arranged to put a slave in the room to watch the mother to make sure she didn't take the boy with her in the middle of the night.

One night during a terrible storm the slave fell asleep. The young woman woke her son and together they walked in the rain to Bayou Bourbeau. The bayou was swollen with rain, and the banks were slick. They tragically slipped into the raging waters and both drowned. Their ghosts are seen walking hand in hand along the banks, especially when it rains.

Over the years several bodies have been found dumped under Marland's Bridge and in the woods on either side.

In the 1970s the body of a teenage girl was found. She had been brutally beaten and then strangled. The murderer was never found. Her wretched spirit has haunted the bridge ever since.

Her apparition is seen standing on the bridge wearing the raincoat she had on the night she was killed. She is also known for turning on the radios of cars passing over the bridge.

It was well after midnight when we arrived at the bridge, which is just a short distance from the plantation. We parked our cars and walked onto the bridge, Tony once again recording audio while the rest of us took photographs.

It was much darker on the bridge than it had been on the battlefield. The trees on either side blocked out what little moonlight penetrated the cloud cover. Rebecca began to sense a presence. She located one spot on the bridge where she would get the sensation of something squeezing her throat each time she stepped into that small area.

I was photographing the bayou from the middle of the bridge, and Rebecca was next to me. Suddenly she screamed and I turned toward her just in time to see a pale grayish shape move quickly to the right. It looked like an outstretched arm. Rebecca asked if I had seen something, and I said yes. She said that when she looked up she saw the ghost of a young woman walk behind me, toward her.

It was early morning by that time so we left. There are several anomalies in my photographs from the bridge. Also, in the photograph that I took on the battlefield, when Natalie's EMF meter pegged, there is a patch of wispy bright red ectomist.

The battlefield of Buzzard's Prairie, Marland's Bridge, and Chrétien Point Plantation are filled with ghosts, some seemingly eager to share their violent past.

The House on Stevenson Street

One of the most frightening aspects of a haunting is the possibility of possession. I am asked about this a lot, and I used to confidently reassure people that I'd investigated hundreds of hauntings and hadn't come across a single case of possession of a living person by a dead person. That changed when I investigated a small house on Stevenson Street in Vinton, Louisiana.

I received a phone call late one evening from a woman who was very upset. She'd had a frightening experience earlier in the day that made her realize that the house she shared with her two small grandchildren was not only haunted but haunted by a particularly nasty ghost.

It's easy to explain away things that are slightly out of the ordinary with "It was just the wind" or "Maybe I forgot to shut that door."

However, when something invisible strikes you physically, there is no explanation, unless you are willing to consider that you might be insane. That is exactly what had happened to the woman earlier that day. She had been sitting on the toilet in her bathroom, with the roll of toilet paper on the floor just in front of her. She reached for it, and it slid across the floor before she could touch it. She sat up, and something hit her across the face, hard. She ran out of the bathroom, literally with her pants down around her ankles.

After a few minutes she calmed down and returned to the bathroom. Nothing appeared to be out of the ordinary, except the large red mark visible on her face. She called her daughter and, Vinton being a small town, was soon given my number.

I lived about a mile from the house at the time, and I did a preliminary investigation that night. I photographed the entire house, inside and out, and interviewed the woman extensively. She was a very credible witness, and it didn't take long for me to realize that the house was haunted and that the family was being severely affected by this.

The woman's grandchildren lived with her, including a granddaughter who was 8 at the time. They had moved into the house during the summer, just before school started. The girl began experiencing emotional problems soon after moving in. She started having temper tantrums, she would shout obscenities, and she was violent toward her brother. When school began she was uncooperative and difficult, and her poor grades reflected her emotional state.

Thinking that the problem had physical roots, she was taken to the doctor, who diagnosed her with ADHD and began drug therapy. Seeing no improvement, the doctor referred her to a psychologist, who added more drugs to the mix. The child was heavily medicated by the time I became involved. Despite the medication she still was having problems at school and sleepwalking.

The sleepwalking began soon after she moved into the house, just as the emotional problems had. The house is laid out in such a way that from the living room you can see through the dining room and kitchen to the back door. The grandmother watched the little girl sleepwalk repeatedly, and each time the girl would attempt to open the back door.

One night the grandmother opened the door for her, without waking her, and the girl walked out the door, down the steps, and across the back yard, up to the edge of a deep canal that runs along one side of the property. The grandmother was horrified, and she led the girl back into the house. The next day she attached a latch with a padlock to the door and it remained locked.

During the three months they had lived in the house, through all the emotional turmoil with the child, other odd things had happened. The children complained that one room in the back of the house, next to the girl's bedroom, was scary and they refused to play in it.

The grandmother had trouble sleeping, and several times late at night while she was in the living room she would hear footsteps in the

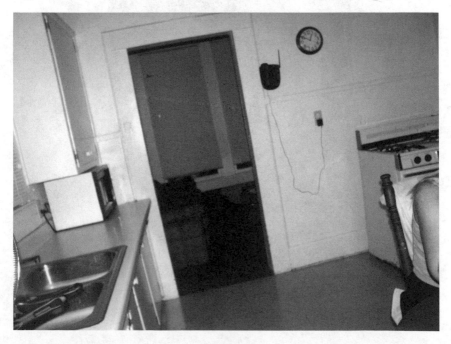

kitchen, only to look up and see no one there. Lights would go on and off by themselves, and the back bedroom where the little girl slept stayed inexplicably cold.

More disturbingly, the girl talked about a man in her room. Sometimes he was a nice man, but sometimes he scared her.

Still, the woman didn't think too much about these things, as they could be explained away as children having overactive imaginations and the creaking of an older house. Until her encounter in the bathroom, that is.

The problems with the child profoundly disturbed me. While I had no personal experience with possession, per se, I had plenty of first-hand experience with the effects a haunting can have on a person's mentality.

It seemed logical to me that the girl was at the very least very upset by the ghost, and was quite possibly manifesting signs of possession, such as the sleepwalking and the personality changes. I kept this to myself that first night, however, and decided to do some digging into the history of the house.

As I mentioned earlier, Vinton, Louisiana, is a small town; it didn't take me long to find people who had information about the house. It was owned by a local man who had bought it from an elderly couple to use as a rental property. The couple lived there for decades, and when they moved out they gave it to their son and his wife. That couple lived there for several years until the wife divorced the man and left with their children. The man remained in the house until he died, in his 40s, from cancer. His parents sold the house soon after.

The house had been rented repeatedly in the interim, with no one staying more than a few months in it.

I could find no record of deaths in the house or on the property. The elderly couple had a good reputation in town, and for the most part so did their son and his family. However, a couple of my friends grew up in a house on that street. They both, independently of one another, told me stories about the elderly couple's son. He had made them both uncomfortable when they were younger with an overly friendly and possibly lecherous manner.

In the meantime the woman had a priest bless the house, which had no effect on the manifestations.

I arranged for a full investigation to be done at the house, with members of the Louisiana Spectral Research Center. We spent several hours taking photographs and shooting video. We were able to capture orbs in still images as well as on video. The majority of the phenomena was captured in the room where the little girl slept.

One of the LSRC members, Beverly Taylor, became extremely nauseated in that room and in the back bathroom, so much so that she had to sit down to regain her composure.

At this point the grandmother asked me what I thought could be done about the haunting, and if I thought that the ghost was affecting her granddaughter. I told her what I had found out about the house and that I thought the ghost was responsible for most, if not all, of the girl's emotional problems.

The woman asked me how to get rid of the ghost. I explained to her that I didn't know how to make it leave, that I didn't know if that was even possible.

She then asked me what I recommended. After several minutes of thought I told her that if my children were involved I would get them out. That is the only time I have advised a family to vacate a house because of a haunting.

The woman sent the children to live with relatives that next day, and she stayed through the week to pack their belongings, then she too moved out. She still had a lease on the place, but she was more than happy to pay rent for the remaining month and live with relatives until she could afford another house.

Immediately after moving out of the house, the little girl changed drastically back to the sweet child she had been before. They took her off all the medications.

Because the woman still had a lease on the house, we were able to do an overnight investigation when she left. After doing another photographic sweep of the house and yard, I decided to sit in the dark in the girl's bedroom. Several other ghost hunters joined me, all with various equipment including video cameras that were recording in infrared.

Not much happened for the first couple of hours, aside from a burning sensation that Beverly Taylor and I both felt on one side of our faces. We were sitting on the floor along the back wall, about three feet from each other, and the sides of our faces that were facing each other were the ones affected.

The video recorders were capturing some anomalies. One member, Ed Jardell, decided to get some sleep in the room next to that bedroom.

I confess that I am very impatient by nature. After hours of sitting in the dark I tend to get a little testy, and this particular ghost was irritating me. I stood up, and told the ghost exactly what I thought of him, out loud. I said that he was a coward who liked to pick on old ladies and children, among other things.

I said that I had made sure that he would never see the little girl again. Still nothing happened, so we left soon after my tirade.

The next morning Beverly Taylor called me. She insisted that I come to Lake Charles to see the video from the night before.

In it there are a few orbs floating around during the hours we sat in the dark room. Then you see me stand up and begin my rant session. Just after I say that the ghost will never see the little girl again, an orb appears in the center of the room and hits me in the chest. I didn't feel anything, but it is clearly visible in the video. The woman who shot the video was so frightened by this that she stopped ghost hunting.

I moved out of Vinton soon after, and I didn't think about the house on Stevenson Street too much in the following years. Then, this fall, an old friend of mine called me. She had just moved into a house a month earlier and was having problems with a ghost. She said, "It's close to your old house, just a block or two over," and I said, "I know exactly which house you're talking about."

Oklahoma City Demon

I don't believe in demons. However, the elderly couple involved in this account certainly does, and maybe it was their strong religious beliefs that targeted them for a diabolical manifestation. Some say that faith shines forth like a beacon through the darkness, and that might explain the sudden, unheralded developments in the quiet little house on 61st Street.

I have changed the names in this account. The couple, both in their 70s when this occurred, was persecuted by the local authorities, the media, and even members of their church after this event.

Harry and Nancy Smith woke up early Sunday morning May 6 to attend church services at the local Pentecostal church. Nancy's brother was the minister there, and the Smiths had been members of the congregation for years. Both Harry and Nancy were devout Christians.

Nancy was taking a bath when Harry heard her scream. He ran into the bathroom and immediately noticed that there was blood on the outside of the bathtub. Assuming that Nancy had hurt herself, he crossed the room and helped her out of the bathtub.

Nancy was very upset, but she hadn't been injured. Then Harry noticed that more blood was on the outside of the tub; indeed it was forming "like beads of sweat" before his eyes. Nancy reached for a towel, and as soon as she touched it the towel became saturated with blood. Blood started to drip down the wall from the mounted heater and ooze from underneath the vanity.

Harry and Nancy were upset and confused by this but not frightened. They decided to go into the bedroom so that Nancy could get dressed. They left the bathroom, and as soon as they stepped into the carpeted hall, blood started to appear on the carpet in front of them. While they watched in amazement, three-toed bloody footprints began to form, leading from the bathroom to the bedroom. In the bedroom, blood appeared on the bed.

The Smiths were afraid now, and they knelt on the floor and started to pray. As they were praying they both felt something sweep by them, moving toward the window. The Smiths felt that the "thing" had left, and there was a sprinkling of blood droplets leading from the bed to the window.

The couple went back to the bathroom. Harry described the room to me as "looking as though someone were bludgeoned." They decided to call the police. The police arrived, interviewed the couple, and took samples of the blood including the towel and a pillowcase to be analyzed.

Somehow the local media got wind of the manifestations, and soon the Smiths were being interviewed by a local television station. The story made the wires, and I was contacted by a television station to give my opinions on the case. I decided to talk to the Smiths directly.

I called the Smiths the next morning. Harry was pleasant and eager to discuss the event with me. He had many questions, and we discussed the possibilities at length. He mentioned stigmata and I assured him that people and religious icons develop stigmata, not furnishings or floors.

I questioned Harry about the history of the house. They had bought the house from friends in 1969. The friends had been the original builders. The house and property had no history of violence or death on the premises, and there was no history of paranormal activity.

The Smiths had been camping the week before at Lake Arbuckle but recalled nothing unusual about the trip. They had been alone in the house all week with the exception of the Avon lady and her daughter who had visited briefly the night before.

Harry wanted me to come to Oklahoma City and personally investigate the incident. I agreed to.

Shortly after my conversation with the Smiths, a representative of the Oklahoma City Police Department called me, unofficially. He had some questions of his own, which I did my best to answer. Then it was my turn. I asked that he fill me in on what he knew.

He confirmed that tests on the substance found in the bathroom had proven to be human blood. He said the bloodstains in the bathroom were confined to a space only two feet off the floor and below, which he found very interesting. He said that the blood was not "arterial" and appeared to be "surface blood that had been oxygenated." He said the blood was "cast off blood" and appeared in a splatter pattern. The blood on the walls appeared to have traveled at a high velocity. There were no seepage marks and the blood was only on the surface fibers of the carpet. The police had thoroughly searched the house and didn't find a container that had held blood or any other physical evidence that the event had been staged.

However, he also said that the police were not ruling out a hoax. They thought that Mrs. Smith may have staged the event either for attention or in an effort to lure more people into attending church. They said that Nancy had an allergy shot twice a week, and therefore had access to syringes. Two syringes were found in the house, but neither contained evidence of ever having held blood.

Nancy and Harry were deeply religious. Nancy told police on the night of the manifestation that "maybe this will bring people back to church." Nancy seemed defensive during questioning, and she quoted the Bible frequently. I asked the police officer if he personally thought that the elderly woman was capable of withdrawing enough blood from herself to cause the stains in the bathroom, bedroom, and hall and he said no.

My second conversation with Harry confirmed a lot of what the police had told me. Harry told me that he and Nancy had been kept at the police station for hours, and that they had been interrogated separately. Harry was amazed that he and his wife were being treated as criminals. They both agreed to do DNA tests to prove that the blood was not theirs.

The next day I called the Smiths again. They had submitted to blood tests. Both of them were very unhappy. The press was hounding them, and indeed the press was hounding me as well, though luckily for me it was only by phone.

I had been asked repeatedly about stigmata, by the press and the Smiths. While I felt that the religious beliefs of the couple definitely came into play, I did not think that this was in any way related to stigmata.

Stigmata is defined as bodily marks or pains resembling the wounds of the crucified Christ and sometimes accompanying religious ecstasy. There have been cases of the personal effects of people afflicted with stigmata manifesting blood, but I didn't think this was the case with the Smiths. The personal effects had all been of profound importance to the afflicted. The Smiths didn't seem to be emotionally attached to the carpet or bathtub.

Historically spontaneous blood formation is associated with murder sites, religious iconography, and demonic visitation. The blood at the Smiths' house was not associated with religious iconography or with the scene of a murder. The Smiths believed that their house had been visited by a demon. Usually demonic visitations are accompanied by feelings of overwhelming terror. When told this, the Smiths said that their faith had protected them from that aspect.

I considered the cases of "rains" of blood and flesh, but none of those events had occurred inside a structure.

The next day I spoke with the Smiths again, and Harry wanted to know if I would still be able to do an investigation of the house. I said yes, I had made plans to be there that weekend. He told me that they wanted no more media involvement, and I didn't blame them. He said that he and his wife felt ostracized by several members of their church.

These people felt that the Smiths must have done something evil in order for a demon to visit them. I told him I understood completely and that I preferred to work without the media.

That afternoon the Oklahoma City Police Department representative called me. He said that the Smiths had just left the station, and that they had been interrogated separately for over two hours. During the interrogation Nancy had asked that the video recorder be turned off and that she had then confessed to staging the event, but would not give any details. I was surprised, and called them.

Harry said that yes, his wife had admitted to staging the event, but only after the detective told her that they were going to prosecute her husband for falsely reporting a crime if they didn't have any answers.

Her confession consisted of her placing her hand on the Bible and saying, "If I did this, I do not remember." Harry said that the police told him that if one of them did not confess, the yard would be dug up in a search for bodies. He said that the detective told them repeatedly to "Just tell us you did it and we'll forget it."

The Smiths were tired of the whole thing by this point. The elderly couple had not been eating or sleeping well. They decided that they just wanted to forget about the whole incident and pretend that it never happened.

Harry asked that I cancel my investigation because he feared that the press would get wind of it. I understood his concerns. He agreed to send me pieces of the carpeting so that I could have some tests done.

I spoke with the Oklahoma Police Department representative again. I asked him for his unofficial thoughts. He said that his supervisors had declined to do DNA tests on the blood because of the high cost of the analysis, but that the blood type, a very common type, matched Mrs. Smith's. He said that several splatter pattern experts had expressed bewilderment at the bloodstains, which had evidently been produced by blood being shot out at a high velocity.

He also said that Harry had never deviated from his account of seeing blood spontaneously form before his eyes. The police officer admitted that he did not think the Smiths were capable of staging the event.

I have communicated with them several times over the years. Each time Harry tells me about the blood again, and his story never changes. He and Nancy believe that they were visited by a thing "of a devilish nature."

I believe the Smiths had an encounter with an unknown entity. I believe in ghosts, so part of me thinks that the religious fervor of the couple attracted the attention of a particularly malevolent ghost that was in turn chased away by the strong beliefs of the couple. Maybe that is the definition of a demon. However, a small nagging part of me wonders if demons do exist, after all.

Pappy

photograph by Greg Stephens

A couple of years ago, three young men contacted the Louisiana Spectral Research Center with an extraordinary account. This led to one of the most unusual hauntings I've investigated.

The young men were out with friends one night when they decided to ride out to Old Camp Road, near Lake Charles, Louisiana. Old Camp Road is a small gravel road literally out in the middle of nowhere, and it is a perfect place to park your car if you want a little…privacy.

The young men and their friends had been drinking beer, but they insisted that they hadn't had much. They parked their trucks on the side of the road, about a mile from the main road. They had been there for about half an hour, some sitting on the tailgate, some walking around, when a couple of them noticed an odd white shape coming toward them from the main road.

They walked slowly toward it, trying to determine what it was. Then they saw that the shape had two red glowing eyes and was moving rapidly down the center of the road toward them.

They ran back to their trucks, got everyone inside, and took off toward the shape, which was between them and the main road.

The shape was still on the road, and just before they reached it, the entity moved quickly to the left side of the road.

The boys and their dates were scared because they had all heard rumors of "Pappy," a ghost that haunted the fields and scrubby woods along Old Camp Road, but until that night they didn't believe the stories.

The stories never said where Pappy came from, although it was assumed that the ghost was associated with either the airfield or the German POW camp that used to be on Old Camp Road.

However, the accounts all describe the same entity—a white adult human-sized shape with glowing red eyes that appeared on the gravel road, and sometimes on the main road in the vicinity.

A few nights later the boys built up their courage and decided to go back and see if the entity appeared again. It was late as they drove slowly down the gravel road. After just a mile or so they became so frightened that they decided to leave. They turned the truck around and headed back to the main road. Suddenly Pappy was in front of them on the gravel road. The driver pushed on the accelerator and sped toward the main road and the entity, which once again moved quickly to the side just in time.

When the boys got home, they noticed that there were long claw marks down the side of the truck. They brought the truck to a body shop to be repaired, and called us to report the incidents. They provided us with a copy of the invoice from the body shop.

When Beverly Taylor first recounted these events to me, I assumed that the boys had been drinking, did something stupid that scratched up the truck, and needed an excuse to tell their parents. However, Beverly said that the boys sounded very scared and sincere, and so the LSRC and I agreed to meet them at a truck stop near Old Camp Road a few nights later. In the meantime, Natalie and Tony Lowery, investigators with the LSRC, researched the area.

Gerstner Field was a World War I aviation training camp. Old Camp Road was once the main thoroughfare through the airfield. They weren't able to find much official reference to the German POW camp reportedly located at Gerstner, but we were able to speak with locals who remembered seeing the German prisoners working in the fields.

Gerstner Field included a 1,120-acre main camp, a 2,230-acre bombing field to the northwest, and a 3,360-acre bombing field to the south. It was one of the largest aviation training camps in the United States. There were over 90 buildings, including 24 aircraft hangers, barracks, shops, and a large YMCA.

Several thousand people worked at Gerstner between 1917 and 1921, and 499 fighter pilots and aviation instructors graduated from its training classes.

There were many accidents and deaths at Gerstner during its short operating period. The aviators were pressured to train quickly, and as a result at least 12 men were killed in aviation accidents.

The most famous, and possibly the most tragic, death was that of Major John P. Mitchell. While flying above the field he went into a sudden maneuver, inverting the plane. He had forgotten to fasten his safety harness and was thrown out of the plane.

The camp was also plagued by flooding and a flu epidemic. On August 6, 1918, Gerstner Field was hit by a hurricane that killed two soldiers and destroyed several buildings and more than 100 planes.

Gerstner Field was closed soon after the end of World War I, and its buildings were either sold or demolished.

I met the members of the LSRC and the three young men at the truck stop. I was also impressed with the boys; they did seem sincere and genuinely frightened and confused as we conducted our interviews. The details of the sightings didn't change as we questioned each one individually. They were scared, but willing to take us to the exact spot where they had seen Pappy.

We followed them to a small, unremarkable gravel road surrounded by fields and thick scrubby trees. We parked and they walked us through the area, pinpointing the location of each sighting.

As we walked with them toward the main road, Malcolm Tillotson and I both noticed something moving in the dense thicket of trees to our left. As we all watched we saw it again; something white was moving through the underbrush. Malcolm, two of the young men, and I rushed into the thicket in an effort to find whatever it was we were seeing.

It was very hard to move quickly through the underbrush, which consisted of thorny trees and briar bushes. To make matters worse,

the terrain was very uneven. The small hills and deep holes were hard to see at night, especially when covered with thick underbrush. We were all bleeding from small cuts and scratches when we found an old ditch that was slightly less over-grown and easier to traverse.

We walked carefully inside the ditch, which thankfully only had occa-sional puddles of water, looking for movement and taking photographs. We didn't see anything else unusual, so we exited the woods near the cars where the rest of

the group was waiting for us. We all decided that this haunting merited further investigation, so we planned to meet again a couple of nights later for a vigil. The boys had had enough by this point and decided not to join us.

We were prepared for our next investigation with boots, lawn chairs, insect repellant, and cameras. I didn't have a digital camera yet, but Jamie Gates, a photographer for the local newspaper, did. We set up our chairs facing each other on the most active section of the road, all of us taking numerous photographs as the night progressed.

After a while Beverly Taylor and I decided to walk around a little. We walked to an opening in the brush that led to a field. We were standing there talking when we both heard a loud, low growl. We jumped, and Beverly grabbed my arm. Then we heard it again. It seemed to come from a small area of tall weeds just to the left of where we were standing. I started throwing rocks into the weeds to try to flush out whatever animal might have been hiding there, and Beverly ran to tell the others. Nothing came out of the weeds, even after the members of the group stomped through the area.

We walked up and down the road, alone and in groups, but Pappy didn't appear. We all settled back down into our lawn chairs. It was a typical Louisiana night—warm, no breeze, and full of insects. The full moon made it easy to see each other and our surroundings.

Movement caught my eye, and I turned to see something very strange moving down the gravel road directly in front of me. It looked like smoke, but it was moving very fast and inside it seemed to be churning. Cigarette smoking is not allowed on our investigations, but I looked to see if anyone was smoking. No one was. Jamie Gates snapped a photograph as I am looking to my right. In it a large wispy mass of ectomist is wrapping around me.

photograph by Jamie Gates

This was the first time I had seen ecto with my naked eye, and it was amazing.

Jamie was able to capture ectomist in a couple of her photographs that night. I had several large orbs in mine, one directly ahead of Beverly Taylor and Ed Jardell, and many bugs. Gregory Stephens had a weird purple and green anomaly in one of his images. Beverly Taylor and Natalie Lowery also had several large bright orbs in their photographs that are definitely not bugs.

Malcolm Tillotson and I decided to go back during the day and scout out the area. We made our way back through the dense underbrush to the ditch, and walked along it for a long way. We soon realized that the bumpy terrain was actually where earth had been bulldozed over old cars and other large debris from the airfield. We found old bottles, tires, and gas cans sticking out of the ground among the thick vegetation.

I still drive down Old Camp Road late at night sometimes, hoping to get a glimpse of Pappy. I drive all the way down to the end of the road and back, careful not to stir up any dust that might keep me from seeing him. I always pause right before I turn onto the main road, hoping to see his red eyes in my rearview mirror. Maybe one night soon he'll appear for me.

The House on Horridge Street

My second husband and I bought an old house soon after we were married. It was built in 1927 and needed a lot of work, but we both loved it and were glad to take on the task. However, soon after the paperwork was signed and work began, we realized that we had bought more than we bargained for.

The first odd thing that we noticed was a brick and concrete structure under the house in the back corner. It looked just like a grave, with a brick bottom and a slab on top. It was being used as a support, so we didn't attempt to see what, if anything, was inside. The second odd thing was that the entrance to the stairwell was boarded up with a large sheet of plywood. We removed the barricade, and the room upstairs became my favorite part of the house.

One huge room with a hardwood floor and windows running the length of three sides and two more on the remaining wall, the room is brilliantly lit by sunlight during the day and moonlight at night. The narrow staircase turned at an angle that wouldn't allow massive furniture to be brought up, so my bedroom set was definitely out. Instead we used one side as my stepdaughter's bedroom and the other side as a playroom.

Tools started disappearing soon after we started renovations. In one instance I was painting one of the bedrooms while standing on a ladder. I climbed down, set my brush down, moved the ladder a little farther along the wall, and turned to get the brush. It was gone. This happened all the time, to the point where we were hesitant to set anything we were working with down. The items would not reappear.

Lightbulbs popped at that house all the time when the switches were flipped on. We chalked it up to old wiring at first, until we had the house completely rewired and new light fixtures put in, and it still happened. Sometimes the bulb would pop so violently that the glass would fly across the room. On two occasions the bulb popped forcibly enough to break the glass holder that it was in.

There was a large porch that wrapped around half the house, from the front door along the side of the living room and dining room to the breakfast room. The breakfast room had a door to the porch. We tore the old flooring off the porch and replaced it.

I was painting the new floor, kneeling by the chimney, when I heard the screen door to the breakfast room open. I could see that side of the porch out of the corner of my eye, and I saw what I thought was my younger son walking toward me. When I looked up to see, he disappeared.

I had seen the ghost of a small boy with dark hair wearing dark pants and a long-sleeved shirt. I realized that he was taller than my son, older by a couple of years.

Then we started having problems with the television sets. We had three—one upstairs, one in the living room, and one in the bedroom that my sons shared. The one upstairs was fine, but the two downstairs would turn on by themselves. Many times I would wake up in the middle of the night to check on the kids and find both television sets on.

The one in the living room would normally display static, and the one in the boys' room would be on a channel, usually BET. More than once I would walk into one of the rooms in time to actually see the television come on and sometimes flip through the channels.

One night in the fall I walked into the bathroom, opened the wall cabinet, and saw a small column of white wispy smoke. It was the approximate size and consistency of steam rising off a cooking pot. It disappeared, and I didn't say anything because frankly I didn't know what to think. I saw it again a few days later in the kitchen, hovering over the counter near the breakfast room, and again in the bathroom near the bathtub.

Then my husband described the same thing to me; he had been seeing it as well. That manifestation only lasted a few months, but was seen both during the day and at night.

I would wake up to check on the kids several times a night because my youngest son has epilepsy. One night as I walked into the bedroom

I saw a dark oval-shaped shadow duck behind the bed, as if trying to hide from me. I took the boys into our room that night.

During all of this the haunting didn't seem malevolent. Creepy yes, but never horrifying or evil. The boys took it in stride, as did my step-daughter when she would visit. Then after a couple of years the activity seemed to escalate, focusing on my older son and his friends.

Several times I came home to find the kids sitting on the porch waiting for me because the ghost was so active. One time my son and a friend were chased out of our living room by the ghost throwing pennies at them from the dining room.

I had surgery during the time we lived in this house, and our neighbor's daughter, Michelle, stayed with me to help around the house. She was in her early teens. One night my husband was cooking dinner and I asked Michelle to take some of my stepdaughter's dolls upstairs, as she had left them in the living room. Michelle took the Barbie dolls upstairs and left them on the dresser, came back down the stairs, and talked to my husband in the kitchen.

She turned to come back into the living room and screamed. I got up as fast as I could and went to her. She and my husband were looking at the stairs: The Barbie dolls had been placed standing on the third step from the bottom. Michelle refused to go back upstairs for a long time, and then eventually she would only go if someone else was with her.

My computer was in the dining room. My chair was against the wall, and the table with my monitor on it faced the open dining room. One night while working I looked up to see a dark tan-colored oval shape, vaguely human-sized, behind the monitor. It sort of leaned toward me, and then disappeared.

Another night while working on the computer, my youngest son, who was three years old at the time, came into the dining room and said, "Ghost." I asked him where the ghost was, and he pointed at the door to his room. It turned out that one of his battery-operated talking toy cars was playing under his bed.

I found it, pulled it out, and tried to turn it off, but the switch wouldn't work, so it continued to make noise.

I used a screwdriver to open up the battery compartment and found that it needed six batteries. Only two were in the compartment, and those two were not touching.

That toy went into the garbage outside that night.

We used to take the children to the beach in Galveston, Texas, leaving early and returning late at night. On one of the visits, after playing at the beach all day, we stopped at the large cemetery in town after dark so that I could take photographs. The kids and my husband stayed in the car as I walked the grounds.

I noticed a Civil War monument; it had a drum carved onto it, among other things. I photographed it and we left. I didn't mention it to anyone, as I didn't think it was of any consequence, and frankly I was tired of interacting at that point.

My older son had two of his friends with him that day, and they both stayed over that night. We were all settled down in bed and I was almost asleep when I heard all the boys screaming, and they came running into my room.

My older son yelled, "My brother, my brother!" and ran back into his room, grabbed my younger son, and ran back. My husband and I were up by this time, and asked what had happened.

As the boys were lying in their room trying to go to sleep, they had all heard a loud rapping on the hardwood floors of the bedroom. My older son and one of his friends were both drummers, and they swore that the sound they heard was someone playing a drum cadence on the floor with drumsticks. I had not told them or my husband one word about the monument I saw earlier that night. They all slept on the floor in my room that night.

My husband and I are no longer together, but he still lives in that house. We have videotaped phenomena moving around the dining room and the boys' room at night with infrared video. We get phenomena on film all the time; in fact it's hard to take a photo at night without capturing something paranormal in it. The lightbulbs still pop, and the televisions still go on and off by themselves. The rest of the activity seems to have quieted down, for now...

Abandoned Buildings

I like abandoned buildings and I've been exploring them since I was a child. I've had many memorable experiences in abandoned buildings, a couple involving pigeons, and a handful involving ghosts.

I grew up in the small town of Vinton, Louisiana. One night when I was in high school my friends and I decided to go into an old house that we knew was empty. The woman who had lived in the house had died a couple of years before, and her family had simply locked up the house, leaving all her possessions inside. We could look into the kitchen window and see dishes still in the sink, and her car was still inside the locked garage.

Three of us went to the house that night. One of us knew the way in—we had to climb onto the roof and then into the attic through a small window. One of us stayed down on the ground as a lookout.

It was really dark in the attic. Even though we only had a small flashlight, we could see that the attic was crammed full of boxes and other stuff.

We were searching around for the door that led into the rest of the house when suddenly a light came on. Hanging from the ceiling was a bare lightbulb with a string as a switch. We looked at each other; neither of us had turned it on, but we turned it off right away, thinking that there must be an electrical short in the wiring. Then we heard our friend outside whistle, so we quickly climbed out of the window and back down to the ground where he was.

We reached him all out of breath, expecting to find that someone else had seen the light in the attic and that we were in trouble. Instead, our friend was just standing there. We asked what had happened, and he said that he could see the lightbulb in the attic when it came on. We said okay, not understanding what the big deal was. Then he pointed at the utility pole. There was no power line running to the house. It had been disconnected.

When I was a teenager one of my favorite abandoned buildings was the Arcade Theater in downtown Lake Charles, Louisiana. The large building had been built at the turn of the century, and many famous people including Houdini performed there when it was a live theater.

It was built during the days of segregation, and the area where black people sat was still there, hard wooden benches above the main floor. There were several private balcony booths at either side of the stage as well, serving the opposite end of the social spectrum.

After live performances went out of fashion, the theater was turned into a movie house. Then when the new Paramount Theater opened just a few doors down, the Arcade was closed completely.

Over the years it was abandoned, and the City of Lake Charles wanted to tear it down to make a parking lot. The Arcade Theater was on the register of historic places, which posed some problems for the city, so it remained standing.

The back entrances to the building were unlocked and vagrants slept in the ticket booth regularly, but they never bothered me and I didn't bother them. I would happily explore the old building for hours, sometimes with friends, sometimes alone.

There were still pianos on the old stage, and behind the stage in the dressing rooms fragments of old movie posters remained on the walls. Underneath the stage and seats was a warren of storage rooms, with props for many of the plays, such as gazebo pieces and wicker furniture.

There was also an old gilded ticket machine lying on its side, too heavy for anyone to take, and boxes of sheet music. Above the stage were several heavy backdrops, and I was able to examine them closely when I felt brave enough to climb a wooden ladder and walk along a narrow wooden catwalk, stepping over the heavy sandbags as I went along.

The first paranormal experience I had at the Arcade involved one of those sandbags. I was on the stage when I heard a dragging sound and then a thud on the stage behind me. One of the sandbags had fallen, missing me by only a couple of feet. I looked up and there was no one on the catwalk, which was completely visible from where I was standing.

Weird things were always happening in the theater. Doors would slam shut by themselves so often that I stopped paying attention. The seats for the audience were the type that folded up when no one was sitting on them, except for one chair on the front row. I had noticed that many times when I was onstage it would be up, or vice versa, but when I went back into the dressing rooms and came back out it would be down, or vice versa. Once I turned around in time to actually see it go down by itself, as if someone were sitting on it.

The projection room was at the front of the theater. There were large movie reels lying around and empty canisters. You could see Ryan Street from a window in the projection room, so it was one of my favorite places to just sit and watch things. Many times my friends and I would be in the projection room and we'd hear noises coming from the stage area in front of us.

Usually we heard knocking sounds or walking, but twice we heard someone playing the piano. You could see the stage and the pianos from our vantage point. Both times the music stopped when we turned to look, and both times no one was on stage.

My most horrifying experience involved the roof of the Arcade. My friend Tony and I had climbed the little ladder from the fire escape to the roof, with me in the lead. I reached the top of the ladder and stepped down onto the roof. Suddenly something flew up from below my feet, and I had to catch myself to keep from falling. I had almost stepped on a pigeon.

The Arcade Theater burned down mysteriously one cold night. The official explanation was that a vagrant had lit a fire on the wooden stage to keep warm. The city got its parking lot.

A few years later I was married and living in Wichita, Kansas. My husband was in the military, and we didn't have much money, but on the weekends we would take long car rides out into the countryside. One Saturday, after exploring for most of the day, we came across an old farmhouse out in the middle of nowhere.

It was a white two-story house with a garage on one side. The house was surrounded by wheat fields and looked anything but spooky with the sun shining on it. We stopped to take a closer look.

We walked up the front steps and discovered that the door was unlocked. Inside we found that the living room was still furnished with an antique-looking sofa, some armchairs, and an upright piano. We quickly toured the inside of the house, finding furniture in all the rooms. In one upstairs bedroom we found a small iron bed completely made, with the covers turned back. Everything was covered in dust and there were dead birds in some of the rooms. Despite the sunlight coming in from the many windows, the house definitely had a very creepy air about it, and we didn't stay inside long.

My husband decided to urinate before we left, and he did this on one side of the garage while I walked around the yard. Suddenly there was a very loud banging sound from the garage, as if someone were pounding on the metal garage doors. It scared my husband so bad that he literally pissed on himself. We both ran back to the car and left.

As I looked back at the house through the dust from the dirt road I saw a dark shadow-shape move between two trees.

Beaumont, Texas, has blocks of abandoned buildings in the old downtown section. They are dangerous to explore, not just because of the usual hazards like rotten floors and pigeons, but also because of the crack addicts that lurk in them.

I have found hypodermic needles, burned dolls hanging from nooses, animal skins, and bloodstains. Most of the old houses contained evidence that vagrants had been living in them at one time or another, the most common thing being rooms carpeted in clothing. Apparently one way vagrants keep warm is to completely carpet an area in deep piles of cloth. Every floor in one house that we explored was completely covered in clothes, two or three feet deep. It was disconcerting.

Usually my friend James and I would be the only ones brave enough (or is that stupid enough?) to enter these houses. We only did so during the day. Luckily we never had any problems with vagrants or crack-heads, and most of the houses were in good shape.

We had systematically worked our way down one street of mostly abandoned buildings over a period of about two weeks, and started on a small side street. There was an old gas station at the end of the street, a vacant lot on the other side of the street, and a huge green house. We decided to come back the next Saturday to explore this house.

We came back with my sister, Wendy, and one of her friends. The house was mostly boarded up, but the back door was unlocked and open. James and I walked into the house. It was surprisingly clean—no clothes on the floor, no graffiti, no evidence that anyone slept in the house or used it for a bathroom.

There was a huge fireplace between two large rooms with the marble mantels still intact. The hardwood floors were barely dusty, and we could see surprisingly well from the exposed tops of the boarded-up windows and from the glass transoms on the front door.

We went up the massive, twisted staircase. I was amazed that no one had looted the house for the ornate woodwork. Even the hardware on the doors remained.

The first landing led to two doors, one on either side. We explored the left side first, and that was when we realized that the house had been turned into apartments at some point. The windows on the upper floors were not boarded up, so bright sunlight lit each room. This apartment looked like it had last been redecorated in the 1970s, with shag carpeting and odd psychedelic wallpaper. We walked around through another door and then we were in the other apartment. It had more of the same carpeting and wallpaper.

We walked out of that apartment and we were back on the landing for the staircase. We went up the remaining flight of stairs. Once again there were two doors leading from the landing. We went into the left one first. This apartment was decorated in more of the 1970s stuff, with an orange bathtub and toilet. However, there was no door at the back of this apartment to the next apartment, so we walked back through to the landing and went through the door on the other side.

This apartment was completely different from the others. The walls were painted a pale yellow, and the paint was peeling off. The floor was bare wood, with old tile in the kitchen and bathroom. The apartment was very bright from the large windows and not spooky at all.

We walked to the room in the front of the house. This room was painted a pale green and had a door that led out onto a balcony over the front porch. The balcony caught our attention immediately, so we went out onto it.

When we turned around and came back in, we were shocked to see that this was the one room in the house with graffiti. Someone had painted a large pentagram on the wall in front of us, with a skull in the center.

I photographed the wall, and we walked back through the next room of the apartment. As we left the room with the pentagram the door slammed shut behind us. We all jumped. We walked through the next room, and that door slammed shut behind us as well. We ran out onto the balcony, and I turned in time to see that door slam shut as well.

We all ran from that house. It was obvious to us now that vagrants wouldn't sleep in that house because it was haunted. As we walked down the street I looked back at the balcony. I didn't see anything unusual, but it kept my attention until I could no longer see it.

That night I had a dream about the house and that apartment. In it a small girl with blond hair was running from room to room, frantic, and then out onto the balcony. I could see an old car in the driveway, and a small boy playing in the yard. I could hear a man and woman arguing.

This dream disturbed me, and when I spoke to James later the next day I told him about it. He was surprised because he had also dreamed about a little blond girl in the apartment, but in his dream she seemed to be mentally disturbed. He said that she was running from room to room and shaking her hands.

I dreamed about the ghost of the little girl for several months after that.

Loyd Hall

One of the more haunted plantations in Louisiana is Loyd Hall, near Cheneyville. William Loyd built it in 1810. William was considered to be a scoundrel by his contemporaries. He was born into the prestigious Lloyd family of London, but his antics embarrassed the family so much that they exiled him to America, giving him enough money to make a new life, but only after he agreed to change the spelling of his last name from "Lloyd" to "Loyd" with one "L."

William settled on the banks of Bayou Boeuf and built himself a fine, two-and-a-half-story home and established a large plantation. The plantation has been in continuous operation since those times, growing cotton, sugarcane, corn, and soybeans on the original 640 acres.

William Loyd and his wife raised an extended family in Loyd Hall, but not without incident. The local Native Americans attacked the plantation several times, and there are still two arrowheads embedded in the front door. There are also bullet holes in the wall of the main hall.

Inez Loyd, William's niece, died after falling from an attic window. It was whispered that she committed suicide after being rejected by her fiancé.

William came to a particularly ignoble end in 1864, one befitting his scandalous reputation. The Union Army used Loyd Hall as a headquarters, and William was pleased to play host, as it saved his plantation from destruction. However, he was soon caught spying for both the Union Army and the Confederate Army. He was summarily tarred, feathered, and hung from one of his own oak trees in the front yard of Loyd Hall.

The Union Army left Loyd Hall soon after William's execution. All but one soldier named Harry, that is. Harry was a violinist and he would play the violin on the balcony in the evenings. He had become infatuated with one of the Loyd daughters, and couldn't bear the thought of leaving her behind, so he hid in the attic.

Mrs. Loyd discovered him one night. Thinking he was an intruder, she shot him. His bloodstains remain on the wooden floor of the attic.

The Loyd family moved out and the building was used as a school for girls before being abandoned completely. It lay empty for years after that, eventually becoming completely overgrown with vegetation.

In 1948 the Fitzgerald family bought the plantation property to use as a pasture for their cattle. They did not know that Loyd Hall was there until they spotted it on one of their visits. The house was completely overgrown with vegetation, and had been used as a barn. Some of the original furnishings, including a rare square grand piano, remained in the house.

The Fitzgeralds cleaned and repaired the beautiful old home, and in 1971 Frank and Anne Fitzgerald moved in with their three daughters. Soon after they moved into the house, the ghosts made their presences known.

The children were the first ones to see "Harry." They were not afraid of the ghost, and considered him to be a playmate. They also became accustomed to seeing the apparition of a black woman wearing an old-fashioned white dress. The Fitzgeralds accept the ghosts as part of Loyd Hall.

The family now lives in a modern home adjacent to the plantation house, which they have turned into a beautiful bed and breakfast. There are cabins behind the main building that also serve as small guest cottages. Several are part of the original plantation complex, and are haunted as well.

The haunting of Loyd Hall manifests in many different ways, and the Fitzgeralds believe that at least four different entities haunt the plantation. Common occurrences inside the house include phantom scents, objects such as silverware disappearing from table tops, lights going on and off by themselves, doors and windows slamming, and rocking chairs moving by themselves.

Staff members once watched a small bowl slide across the dining room table, seemingly of its own volition. Auditory phenomena are also common at Loyd Hall, including phantom piano music, screams, and wisps of conversation.

The ghosts are active in the guest cottages behind the main house as well. The ghost in Cottage 4, which is the old commissary, likes to shake the bed, and more than one guest has left in the middle of the night after being awakened by the sensation of someone kicking the

bed. Guests in the Camellia Cottage have reported watching the doors to the old armoire open and close by themselves. One guest left after seeing a door violently fly off its hinges.

I initially scouted Loyd Hall as a possible location for MTV's *Fear* television program. The history and level of ghostly activity were great for our purposes, but the overall area was a little smaller than we wanted. However, I was impressed with the haunting and I enjoyed talking to the staff and the Fitzgeralds.

I was contacted by a local television station in the fall of 2003 about filming an investigation in a plantation. Loyd Hall was one of my top recommendations. Rick with WJTV out of Mississippi contacted the Fitzgeralds, and soon I was driving to Cheneyville to meet the small production staff for an overnight ghost hunt.

I arrived at Loyd Hall just before sunset. Fields of sugarcane surrounded the house. The brown waters of Bayou Beouf were already becoming shrouded in fog. Rick, the producer, met me outside and introduced me to the rest of the team: Jeff, the on-air personality, Dave, the director, and Rob, the cameraman. Rick, Dave, and Jeff all shot video as well.

We carried most of my gear upstairs to the suite in which I would be sleeping. The guys eventually slept in the cottages outside. However, most of the night was spent investigating the house and the grounds.

We did an initial camera sweep, in which I used my digital camera to look for phenomena in an effort to pinpoint hot spots on which to focus later. It was still early, and I didn't get much, just a faint orb on the second-story balcony. We paid special attention to the attic room containing the bloodstains and to the small attic spaces where Harry spent the last few days of his life hiding, but we had no luck.

It was dark by this time, so we went outside and did a thorough sweep of the grounds. We walked down to the bayou and then back up the lawn to the house. I captured orbs on my digital camera near the large magnolia trees, and was able to track it in successive frames as it moved erratically between the trees and the house. There are several unmarked graves on the property, and we were near two of them.

We went back inside to the back informal dining area and had delicious sandwiches and snacks prepared for us by the staff of Loyd Hall. The staff left and we sat at the table and talked for an hour or so. Then

we all heard a loud creaking noise from the hall leading to the front door. We jumped up and ran to see what might have caused it but found nothing.

Taking that as our cue to begin, I went through the entire house turning off lights. We would investigate in darkness.

We systematically explored each room on the bottom floor of the house, and then moved up to the second floor. We had walked from one suite to the other when Rob noticed a strong perfume scent. All of us could smell it, but only in a very small, localized area in one bedroom. Then it moved. The concentrated odor moved across the hall to the suite where I would be sleeping. It seemed to linger there for a few minutes, and then it proceeded to the front bedroom. It stayed in that one room for the rest of the night, although it would move from one side to the other.

The odor was very strong; we could literally walk in and out of the small area and tell the difference. It was a very sweet, floral scent, like perfume or a large mass of flowers. We were amazed that we could follow the scent from one room to the next, especially as it crossed the large hall, one end of which has a door that opens onto a balcony.

We searched the house for an explanation, although we knew nothing would explain the movement. The only flowers inside were in a large arrangement downstairs, but they were old and did not smell at all. We searched outside and there were no blooming plants.

We went back inside. Rob and I focused on the bedroom with the odor while Dave, Jeff, and Rick went up to the attic.

I set up my video camera in infrared mode to film in darkness, and Rob was filming in infrared as well. Then we both started taking still photographs with our digital cameras. Soon we isolated an area near a large full-length mirror that had activity.

Suddenly we started to get clouds of orbs in our photographs, simultaneously. We were picking them up on video as well. The orb clusters were huge, and we could track them in successive shots as they moved away from the mirror and toward us. Just as suddenly the orbs would disappear, leaving only one or two faint anomalies, then bam, the cluster would appear again.

I have taken thousands of photographs in haunted places. I have photographed clusters of orbs before. However, I have never captured clusters of that size and intensity, or that behaved in that manner. The manifestations seemed to focus on Rob and me, and I was able to entice

the entity into moving closer to me by holding out my hand. Rob captured the movement in his still images, but when he tried to videotape it the camera refused to focus, and he could see a dark shadowy mass moving between the camera and me.

While we were capturing phenomena on the second floor, Jeff, Rick, and Dave had an odd encounter in the attic. The small spaces under the eaves of the house are blocked off from the rest of the attic, with two small doors giving access for storage.

The guys looked in one, shot some video, and didn't see anything unusual, so Jeff latched the door back and they went to the other side of the attic and opened the small door there. When they came back through to the stairs they noticed that the first door was open again. Jeff had securely latched it, and none of them had opened it again.

After over an hour of photographing the phenomena in the bedroom, the activity seemed to decrease until eventually only small, faint orbs were visible in our images. By this time it was well after 3 a.m., so we decided to call it a night. The guys set up a video camera in the hall outside my room and locked me in the plantation alone.

I got ready for bed and turned out all the lights, expecting a ghostly encounter of some sort. Maybe Harry would serenade me with his violin, or Inez would play the piano. If I was lucky Sally might tuck me in, or William would appear coated in feathers. However, the only visitor I received that night was a very friendly house cat, which jumped onto the bed and slept beside me. I soon fell asleep and slept soundly until Rick knocked on the door the next morning.

The video camera outside my door did pick up what sounded like women talking, but it is so faint that we cannot discern what they are saying. At one point just before dawn the camera tries to focus on movement in the hall, but was unable to.

Loyd Hall is a delightful place. The staff is gracious and friendly and it seems that the ghosts are as well. I intend to go back and further my investigation. Maybe next time the ghosts will be even more accommodating.

Ghost Photography Techniques

Capturing ghost photographs is easy once you learn a few basic techniques. All you need is a camera or a video camera and an active haunted location.

Still photography techniques

- Take photos in no light or low light, using a flash.

    Because you are more likely to get positive results with your photography in the dark, it is necessary to use a flash. However, be aware that using a flash has disadvantages. The light from the flash can cause weird anomalies in your images as it bounces off of shiny surfaces such as mirrors, windows, glossy walls, and moisture. You can minimize these effects if you adjust your flash settings. If you are photographing outdoors at night or in a large open space, such as an auditorium, change your flash settings to high. Alternately, if you are photographing in a narrow space, such as a dark hallway or a small room, change your flash settings to low. If you are unable to adjust your flash settings, just be especially aware of your surroundings and how they might affect your results.

- Take photos with people in them.

    Ghosts seem to be attracted to living people, and many of the best ghost photographs were captured inadvertently with living people as the intended subjects. Keep that in mind while photographing haunted places. Many ghosts also seem to be interested in animals.

- Take photographs behind you.

    Have you ever had the feeling that something was following you, especially as you walked down a dark staircase or hallway? Ghosts like to follow people, and even sneak up on them. Some of my best photographs were taken after I had investigated an area, walked out, and then turned to take one more photograph.

- Talk to ghosts as you investigate.

  Many ghosts seem to respond to interaction with the living. Investigators get great results by talking to ghosts out loud as they photograph.

- Watch for artifacts in front of your lens.

  Most photographs of "vortices" are actually camera straps or hair fibers in front of the camera lens. Therefore, be sure to either remove your camera strap or wear it around your neck. Also remove any lens cap straps. If you have long hair, pull it back.

- Concentrate on areas that elicit an emotion from you, such as sadness, anger, fear or even joy.

  Many people seem to be able to sense ghosts. Sometimes an otherwise unassuming area can make you feel uncomfortable or can inexplicably catch your attention. Focus on those areas.

- Do not consume alcohol during an investigation.

  Not only can it make you careless and more prone to accidents, but it also makes you an unreliable witness to whatever phenomena you may encounter.

- Do not smoke during an investigation.

  Smoke looks like ectomist in photographs. One person smoking anywhere in the vicinity of ghost photography compromises the integrity of all results.

- Watch for light pollution.

  Avoid taking photos with sources of light in them, such as streetlights, headlights, flashlights, etc. I have seen numerous "ghost photographs" that are really just streaks caused by lights in the background.

- Avoid taking photos when it is raining, snowing, or foggy.

  These conditions are responsible for more false positives in ghost photography than any others. The flash on your camera bounces off the particles of moisture.

- Avoid taking photographs when it is excessively dusty. Dust particles in the air can result in the same flash bounce-back anomalies as moisture particles.

- When investigating outdoors, be sure to thoroughly photograph any structures in the area.

  Ghosts like buildings. Even if the structure isn't directly associated with the haunting, if it is in the immediate area it might be haunted as well. For example, caretaker's shacks in cemeteries are a good place to photograph.

- Hold your breath when it's cold.

  One of the most important things to remember when you are photographing in cold conditions is to hold your breath when you snap the photo. A good rule of thumb is to exhale and count to three before taking the photograph.

- Take test shots with your camera equipment.

  It is important to see what sort of results your camera will get with moisture, dust, etc., so that you can ascertain the difference in your photographs. Take photographs of fog, rain, and snow. Place dust on your lens and take several shots. Take photographs of breath on a cold night, smoke, anything that might resemble a ghost in the photographs you take during an investigation.

- Be sure to photograph the gate or entrance as you depart an investigation.

  Many ghosts are curious and will follow you. Tell the ghosts that this is their last chance to be photographed as you leave; many times they will manifest in the last shots.

- Avoid taking photos of huge open areas.

  Camera flashes have a hard time illuminating dark open spaces. For example, instead of photographing in the middle of a field, have something fairly close in your shot, such as a tree, structure, or gravestone.

Video

Many of the same rules apply to video photography as to still photography. However, there are some additional tips to follow:

- In order for the video camera to "see" the phenomena in very low light you must use some form of illumination. While I have seen results with the standard video camera light, the most effective way of lighting up an area is with an infrared light source and filter.

    Many video cameras come equipped with this under various names, such as Nightshot. You will know that you are in this mode when the images in your viewfinder appear to have a greenish tint. Some video cameras also have a super infrared option that slows down the shutter speed in addition to using an infrared light and filter. I do not recommend using this option, as the slow shutter speed slows down the video. Many times the standard infrared light provided by the manufacturer is not bright enough for large areas. I recommend purchasing an external infrared light that mounts onto your video camera.

- While it is possible to capture phenomena on video while walking through an area, it is more likely that you will get positive results if your video camera is stationary. Ghostly phenomena usually moves quickly, and if the camera is still it can be recorded more effectively. I suggest choosing an active spot and mounting the camera on a tripod or placing it on a level, flat surface and leaving it to record while you investigate the rest of the area. If you must carry the video camera, be sure to move slowly and smoothly throughout the area.

Orbs

Orbs are the most controversial paranormal subject. Every ghost hunter has an opinion about whether or not the translucent round photographic anomalies are paranormal in nature. Many experts say that orbs are simply lens flares, the camera flash bouncing off moisture or dust particles, or other photographic errors.

Indeed, those experts are right—most of the time.

However, not all orbs can be so easily explained. When I meet another investigator I always ask them what they think orbs are. I use it as a sort of litmus test. If the ghost hunter tells me that all orbs are merely photographic errors or lens flares, then I know that particular ghost hunter does not actively investigate. Anyone who is out in the field gathering evidence regularly knows that not all orbs can be explained rationally.

Orbs

photograph by Aron Boyle

Orbs are present at hauntings. I cannot say for certain that ghosts manifest as orbs. However, I have photographs of clouds of orbs seemingly transforming into ectomist. Orbs are in many photographs of other ghostly phenomena.

It is the behavior of orbs that intrigues me. Many times I have tracked them with my digital camera as they circle around me or move along hallways or through tombstones. I have even photographed them as they moved closer to my outstretched hand. Orbs seem to interact with people and with the environment.

Even the most diehard skeptic cannot explain the orbs caught on video. The footage of orbs streaming in and out of haunted places and moving of their own accord is as exciting as it is important. Particles of moisture do not move of their own volition against air currents. Dust particles do not appear in clusters that remain static for several minutes, then zoom away only to reappear moments later in another area.

Keep all this in mind when you look at your photographs. That odd transparent round anomaly next to your grandmother might just be the ghost of your dead grandfather.

Acknowledgments

I'd like to thank all my ghost-hunting friends, including Beverly Taylor, Tony and Natalie Lowery, Rebecca Brown, Keith Age, Debe Branning, James Wardrop, Kalila Smith, Chris and Ginger Pennell, and Malcolm Tillotson. Thanks to Andy and Kim Mills for the fantastic Gettysburg photographs. Thanks to Kelly Wardrop for commiserating.

Thanks to Mark Christoph for sharing his photographs and for enthusiastically traipsing through cemeteries, abandoned buildings, hurricanes, and other inhospitable locations with me.

Thanks to my partner in crime, Chester Moore, for the inspiration.

Thanks to my mom, Rose McBride, for the pep talks and the proofreading.

Thanks to Cade Stephens, my youngest son, for dealing with a very busy and eclectic mommy. Thanks to Greg Stephens for lending a helping hand. Thanks to my grandmother, Bernice LeBlanc, for providing a very haunted house for me to grow up in. Thanks to my extended family Putt, Zach, and André.

Thanks to the members of Paranormal.com for the inspiration to continue searching for the answers.

Thanks to R. Travis Beck and Shane Garner for being patient enough to photograph a photographer.

Thanks to Cris Abrego, Tod Dahlke, Rick Telles, Roberto Cardenas, Carl Hanson, and the other crew members of MTV's *Fear*.

Thanks to Mitchel Whitington for the opportunity to write this book and to my publisher, Ginnie Bivona, for listening.

Thanks to Aron Boyle, my oldest son, for dealing with the late-night editing sessions, critiquing my work, and always supporting everything I do. I love you.

Special thanks to Dana Basken for his daily encouragement and enthusiasm and for consistently telling me to "go write your book and stop procrastinating."

I'd like to thank Jeff Taylor for going that extra mile by reading all my work and even becoming possessed during an investigation. This book would not be here without his love and support.

Finally, I'd like to thank my dad, Daniel C. LeBlanc. I miss you.

Bibliography

www.uss-hornet.org
http://www.hauntedbay.com/features/usshornet.shtml
http://www.missioncreep.com/mw/estate.html
http://www.prairieghosts.com/waverly_tb.html
http://www.waverlyhillstbsanatorium.com/
http://www.lungsandiego.org/lung/kids_tb_history.asp
http://www.tranquilleonthelake.com/
http://www.selfadvocatenet.com/about_us/history.asp
http://www.wabash.lib.in.us/murder.htm
http://www.sapiparanormal.com/
http://www.prairieghosts.com/b-cave.html
http://www.subversiveelement.com/BellWitchofTennessee.html
http://www.johnsrealmonline.com/paranormal/bellwitch/history.html
http://www.civilwarhome.com/stonesriver.htm
http://www.vectorsite.net/twcw36.html
http://ngeorgia.com/history/chickam.html
http://www.militaryhistoryonline.com/civilwar/chickamauga/
    dayone.aspx

The Encyclopedia of Ghosts and Spirits by Rosemary Ellen Guiley
Strange Tales of the Dark and Bloody Ground by Christopher K.
    Coleman
Haunted Louisiana by Christy L. Viviano
Ghosts Along the Bayou by Christine Word
Journey Into Darkness: Ghosts and Vampires of New Orleans by Kalila
    Katherina Smith
The Haunted Realm by Simon Marsden

Look for these titles in the *Haunted Encounters* series:

Haunted Encounters: Real-Life Stories of Supernatural Experiences

ISBN 0-9740394-0-3

Haunted Encounters: Ghost Stories from Around the World

ISBN 0-9740394-1-1

Haunted Encounters: Personal Stories of Departed Pets

ISBN 0-9740394-2-X

Release May 2005

Haunted Encounters: Living in a Haunted House

ISBN 0-9740394-6-2

Release March 2005

Haunted Encounters: Departed Family and Friends

ISBN 0-9740394-3-8

Other Books by Atriad Press

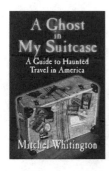

A Ghost in My Suitcase:
A Guide to Haunted Travel in America

by Mitchel Whitington

Available March 2005
ISBN 0-9740394-5-4

Staci's Guide to Animal Movies

by Staci Layne Wilson

Available June 2005
ISBN 0-9740394-8-9

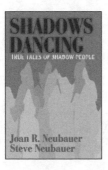

Shadows Dancing:
True Tales of Shadow People

by Joan and Steve Nuebauer

Available June 2005
ISBN 0-9740394-7-0

For ordering information

www.atriadpress.com

Atriad Press LLC
13820 Methuen Green
Dallas, TX 75240
972-671-0002